William Graham Sumner

Lectures on the history of protection in the United States

Delivered before the International Free-Trade Alliance

William Graham Sumner

Lectures on the history of protection in the United States
Delivered before the International Free-Trade Alliance

ISBN/EAN: 9783337284275

Printed in Europe, USA, Canada, Australia, Japan

Cover: Foto ©ninafisch / pixelio.de

More available books at **www.hansebooks.com**

LECTURES

ON THE

HISTORY OF PROTECTION
IN THE UNITED STATES

DELIVERED BEFORE THE INTERNATIONAL FREE-TRADE ALLIANCE

BY

W. G. SUMNER

PROFESSOR IN YALE COLLEGE

NEW YORK
PUBLISHED FOR THE
NEW YORK FREE TRADE CLUB
By G. P. PUTNAM'S SONS
27 & 29 WEST 23D STREET
1883

Press of
G. P. Putnam's Sons
New York

PREFACE.

The following lectures were delivered by me before the International Free Trade Alliance, in New York, in the spring of 1876. They are here republished exactly as delivered, although there are certain points which I should like to elaborate, if the opportunity were offered. I have endeavored here to combine two things: 1st, the history of our own tariff legislation, showing its weakness, ignorance, confusion, and oscillation; and, 2d, a discussion of the arguments for and against free trade, as they have presented themselves in the industrial and legislative history of the country. I have summed up in the last lecture the convictions to which such a study of the subject must lead. Suffice it here to say, that when one clears one's head of all the sophistries and special pleas by which protection is usually defended, and looks at the matter as a simple matter of common sense, one must be convinced that an industrious people on a fertile soil, so abundant in extent that population is inadequate to the highest organization of labor, must enjoy advancing wealth and prosperity. They will owe this to a diligent use of their natural advantages. They will reach the maximum of production when they produce and exchange most freely. Certainly no application of taxation can possibly increase their production ; that is their national wealth. Every tax or other interference with the freedom of production or exchange produces restraint, confusion, delay, change, risk and vexation, and these, as every one knows, cause loss of time, labor, and capital, that is, diminish the product which may be obtained from a given amount of labor. The amount of this loss can never be measured in figures, because we can never get statistics of "what might have been ;" but when it is shown here that the legislation of the United States has been constantly vacillating, not only in its policy, but also in the degree to which its policy has been pursued; that it has laid burdens on production and exchange in a clumsy, brutal, and ignorant disregard of possible effects on the delicate network of modern industry; that it has had in view, from point to point, only a single interest, and has had no national stand-point or conception of the public interest (much as it boasts to the contrary) ; then, I think, any one must see that such legislation has lamed the national productive power, wasted the natural advantages which the nation enjoys, diminished its wealth, and contracted the general status of comfort for the whole people.

Adam Smith laid down four rules by which all taxes ought to be tested. Experience has ratified them so thoroughly that they are no longer questioned by anybody. They ought to be known by everybody.

1. Taxes should be, as far as practicable, equal.
2. They should be definite in amount (not uncertain or variable).
3. They should be collected, so far as possible, at the time most convenient to the payer, so as not to cripple the process of production.
4. They should be so arranged as to give the maximum revenue to the government at the minimum cost to the people, *i. e.*, they should cost as little as possible to collect; and they should keep capital out of the hands of the people as short time as possible.

Protective taxes are hostile to revenue, because the purpose of a protective tax is to prevent importations. The moment, however, that a tax begins to have this effect it prevents revenue. Hence, *where protection begins, there revenue ends.*

There is no conceivable ground of right by which the legislature may decide what things ought to be produced, and in what measure, and then use its taxing power to carry out its notions. Every tax is an evil, and it is on the defensive. Its need must be shown, and *no tax can be defended which is laid for anything but revenue to defray the legitimate and necessary cost of public peace, order, and security.*

For taxes laid to this end, some further rules can now be laid down as established by long experience.

1. No such taxes should be allowed to act protectively to any degree. They should be offset by excise taxes of equivalent amount.
2. They should be laid on as few articles as possible, and in the simplest way possible (to avoid expense in collection).
3. The legislator should try to find the maximum revenue point on each article (*i. e.*, If there were no tax there would be no revenue. If there were a prohibitory tax there would be no revenue. There is a point between, at which the highest revenue can be obtained with the least cost and the least fraud).
4. Raw materials should not be taxed. (It is not easy to define "raw materials," but the rule has value as a practical rule. Taxes on raw materials strangle industry at its birth.)

These rules are only practical rules, derived from experience. There are no scientific laws of taxation, because there are no natural laws of taxation. Nature has not provided for taxation, as she has for production, exchange, distribution, and consumption. Taxation is part of the co-operation of society for its own defense against the evil and destructive forces within itself. Any state which lays protective taxes misuses the means of defense to increase the evils.

W. G. S.

CONTENTS.

LECTURE I.
THE NATIONAL IDEA AND THE AMERICAN SYSTEM,

LECTURE II.
BROAD PRINCIPLES UNDERLYING THE TARIFF CONTROVERSY,

LECTURE III.
THE ORIGIN OF PROTECTION IN THIS COUNTRY,

LECTURE IV.
THE ESTABLISHMENT OF PROTECTION IN THIS COUNTRY,

LECTURE V.
VACILLATION OF THE PROTECTIVE POLICY IN THIS COUNTRY—CONCLUSION,

LECTURE I.

THE NATIONAL IDEA AND THE AMERICAN SYSTEM.

It is a sign of a dogma in dissolution to change its form and to yield points of detail, while striving to guard its vested interests and traditional advantages. Just now the dogma of protection is striving to find standing ground, after a partial retreat, for a new defense, in the doctrine of nationality. We are told that there is only a "national" and not a "political" economy, that there are no universal laws of exchange, consequently no science of political economy; that it is only an art, and has only an empirical foundation, and that it varies with national circumstances to such a degree as to be controlled by nothing higher than traditional policy or dogmatic assumption. Great comfort is found for this position in the assertion that the German economists have discovered or adopted its truth. How utterly unjust and untrue this is as a matter of fact, those who have read the works of the German economists must know. It is untrue, in the first place, that they are unanimously of the school of the *socialistes en chaire*, and, in the second place, it is untrue that the *socialistes en chaire* are clear and unanimous in their position. They occupy every variety of position, from extreme willingness to entrust the state with judgment in the application of economical prescriptions, to the greatest conservatism in that regard. Finally, it is not true that any of them are protectionists.

We do not intend, however, to discuss the opinion or authority of the schools in question. If it should be claimed that the extreme admission made by some of the Germans of this school, that protection may be beneficial to a nation at a certain stage of development, is applicable to the United States to-day, we should desire no better footing for the controversy.

It is more directly interesting, however, to examine the doctrine of nationality on its merits. It will appear upon even a cursory examination of this kind, that existing nations are arbitrary and traditional divisions. There was published in Europe, in 1863, when the Emperor Napoleon was urging on an attempt to secure stable equilibrium in European politics by adjusting political divisions according to race and language divisions, a map of Europe thus rationally constructed. The effort, however, offered the most striking proof of the impossibility of reconstructing, on any such rationalistic or logical basis, political circumstances which are the historical outgrowth of political struggles and political accidents. The nations which must be made the subject of discussion are, therefore, such as exist, and of them it is true that their boundaries coincide with no lines of race, language, culture, industry, commerce, or anything else which would give the basis of scientific classification, so that different principles could be consistently applied in each. There was a time, indeed, when the civil subdivisions were small and numerous—when manners, customs, costumes and language varied over every hundred square miles of Europe—but the whole tendency of the great inventions of modern times is to obliterate these boundary lines for purposes of industry and trade.

It is not necessary to go into the history of Europe for proofs and illustrations. The very best are furnished by our own continent and our own nation. The geographical area known to-day as the United States is the result of discovery, conquest and purchase. It would have been impossible a century ago to constitute an empire of such extent, and to govern it according to the requirements of modern life. The improvements in transportation and the transmission of intelligence have made it physically possible, and the combination of local institutions with a centralized organization has made it politically possible.

When we turn to inquire, however, why it has been limited just as it has, why Canada and Mexico are outside, and why Texas, California and Alaska are within, we come at once to the historical antecedents which are partly accidents and partly ancient struggles and hostilities. Canada was never made thoroughly English before the revolutionary war; while it was French it was always hostile to the English colonies. This hostility was traditional, and there was no sympathy with the revolution. New Brunswick and Nova Scotia were largely peopled by the Tory refugees, whom the unwise severity of the Whigs forced to emigrate during and after the war. Texas was won from Mexico in war. California and the other Pacific States were obtained partly by conquest and partly by purchase. A few years ago we discussed a plan for purchasing San Domingo. Out of these historical movements, part of which fell out one way and part the other, the actual geographical limits of the United States result.

Now, according to the Constitution of the United States, no one of these States can make any laws restricting commerce between itself and any of the others. If it be asserted that states which pursue different industries cannot afford to trade freely with one another, here we have them—New York and Pennsylvania, Massachusetts and Minnesota, Maine and Louisana. If it be asserted that states with like industries cannot afford to trade freely with one another, here we have them—Indiana and Illinois, Iowa and Minnesota, Massachusetts and Rhode Island, Alabama and Mississippi. If it be said that small States cannot afford to trade freely with great empires, here are New York and Connecticut, Pennsylvania and Delaware. Why do not the great states suck the life out of the small ones? If it be said that new states with little capital, and on the first stage of culture, cannot afford to exchange freely with old states having large capital and advanced social organization, here are New York and Oregon, Massachusetts and Idaho. How can any territories ever grow into states under the pressure? If it be said that a state which relies on one industry cannot afford to exchange freely with one which has a diversified industry, here are Pennsylvania and Colorado, California and Nevada, any of the cotton states and any of the north-eastern states. No such strong illustrations are furnished by any states in the world which are sovereign and independent of each other. The Constitution of the Union enforces absolute freedom of exchanges, and each state pays its own taxes and supports its own government. The traveler rarely knows when he passes from one state to another. As to what he buys or where he buys, what he sells or where he sells, it would be considered an unwarrantable impertinence for any public official to inquire. Yet no man has ever been known, so far as we are aware, to complain of this as a hardship, or as imposing a loss upon him, and no such complaint has arisen from any state as a state, nor has any one been heard to claim that there was here an actual loss, which must be endured for the sake of the great benefits which come from Union. On the contrary, it is universally and tacitly agreed that this is one of the great benefits of the Union.

Here, however, comes in another phase of the matter. If a man lives in Vermont he must trade freely with New Hampshire, Massachusetts and New York, but if he wants to trade northward to Canada, it is regarded as fatal to him and to his country, that he should do so freely. As we won Texas from Mexico, we enter into absolute free trade with her, but we think that it would be ruinous to trade freely with the rest of the ancient state of Mexico. If we had got the political jurisdiction of San Domingo, we should have entered into free exchanges with her, but the difficulty of the political jurisdiction was the main ground of the wise decision of the nation not to buy that island. If, however, we cannot have the trouble of the political jurisdiction, we think it would be calamitous to have the free exchanges. Free exchanges with Cuba are not to be thought of on our part, even if they would be granted on hers.

Here, then, the refutation of the "nationality" notion is right before us, and it is at the same time the condemnation of our policy in regard to foreign commerce. If there be any such thing as an "American system"—a system which we can claim to illustrate and advocate before the civilized world, it must be that of absolute free trade, each state or nation providing for its own needs and expenses, each state freely open to all comers, securing peace and safety to persons and property while within its borders.

The "British system" is different, and is distinctly defined. It is to raise revenue by customs for convenience, and to lay excises to counteract "incidental protection." We would be very glad to see the British system introduced into this country, but if the protectionists taunt free-traders with flinching from the consequences of their doctrine, we accept the challenge. We are convinced by the experience of the United States, that the best system would be to have absolutely free exchanges, and to leave each nation to pay the expense of maintaining the organization of society within its own borders.

Another application of the facts here discussed which is put to us, is deserving of far less respectful treatment. It is said that we have free trade already within the Union, and that we are discontented and unreasonable, because we demand more. It would be difficult to show why a man who has ten thousand dollars should not sue for ten thousand more which are due him, or why a man who enjoys the right of locomotion is unreasonable in demanding the right of association.

There is in all that we have said no infringement upon the true idea of the "nation," and no derogation from its value and dignity. It exists historically and traditionally. and we take it as it is handed down to us. It is an organized human society, whose limits are given historically, and are maintained for convenience, because they allow play to certain local interests, prejudices, traditions, habits and customs. Whether it is formed by accident and immemorial tradition, or by colonization and legislative act, it develops an organic life. The society as such develops functions. Its harmonious action emanates from its individual members and reacts upon them. Its government is the machinery by which harmony, co-operation and unity are brought about. It would seem, however, that America had done its greatest service to the world by showing that states did not exist for the sake of bringing men into convenient groups for making either commercial or military war upon each other, but that they might more easily embrace the earth in a family of harmonious communities.

LECTURE II.

BROAD PRINCIPLES UNDERLYING THE TARIFF CONTROVERSY.

The world has heard a great deal about liberty for the last century. That period has been marked by great struggles on the part of nations to secure independence, and on the part of classes and individuals to secure freedom from old traditional restraints. The world has struggled towards "freedom" and "liberty" as if these were the first considerations of peace, justice, prosperity and happiness, and the result has been to produce, in the forefront of modern civilization, states whose fundamental principle is to give the freest scope to individual energy and effort.

We in the United States make it our greatest boast that we have accepted this broad principle absolutely, and applied it fearlessly; nevertheless, we, who are met here to-night, are associated to demand more liberty. There is no body of our fellow-citizens worth mentioning who deny the right and the expediency of private property. What we have to demand, and what the majority of our fellow-citizens—so far as their will has yet been constitutionally expressed—deny us, is the privilege of using our property as we like, that is, of exchanging it when and where and with whomsoever we will. When we demand this privilege, which belongs to us on the simplest principles of right reason and common sense, we are met by a speculative theory based on artificial assumptions, put forward sometimes on bare considerations of selfish interest, and sometimes with no little parade of abstract philosophizing. We are told, "Oh, no! It is not best for the state that you should do as you like about making your exchanges. The legislature must consider the question, and prescribe for you with whom and for what you shall exchange. If you deal with the designated persons, your countrymen, they will gain, the wealth of the community will increase, and you, as a member of the community, will participate, and be better off in the end than if you had been let alone."

Now, we dispute this theory at every stage. We deny that the state, *i. e.*, the legislature, can make any such provision for us better than we can make for ourselves, and we appeal to experience of everything it tries to do; we deny that it has any business to theorize for us in the premises; we deny that the designated persons will gain—at least, that they will gain as much as they would if they were left to deal with us on their own footing; we deny that they can gain anything from us, *on account of the law*, but what we lose; we deny that the total gains to one part of society by this process can ever exceed the total losses of another part, *i. e.*, that the process can increase the wealth of the community; we deny, finally, that our share of these hypothetical gains can ever be redistributed to us so as to bring back our first loss. We have never seen money go through such a process, passing through many hands, and come back whole, to say nothing of loss and waste.

Thus the issue is joined. On the one side are broad and simple principles, so elementary that they are mere truisms, and on the other side are special pleas of various kinds set up to befog men's judgment, and prevent them from drawing the inferences which follow inevitably.

Let me suggest to you two or three of the broadest and most commanding principles which really decide this question:

1. We, Americans, have made it the first principle of our society that no man shall obtain by law any advantage in the race of life on account of birth or rank, or any traditional or fictitious privilege of any kind whatsoever, and on the other hand, we have removed, so far as the law can remove, all the hindrances and stumbling blocks which come from circumstances of birth and family. Society gives no aid, but it removes all obstacles of social prejudice and tradition. There is not a man in the country who does not respond with a full heart to the wisdom and truth of this relation of society to the individual. Now, on what principle is this relation based? It is on the belief that society makes the most of its members in that way. Some men have more in them than others. We do not know which is which until they show it; but we believe that the way to let each one come to his best, is for society to set them all on their feet, and then let them run each for himself. We believe that the best powers of the community are brought out in that way.

It does not follow that men so treated never make mistakes, and never ruin themselves. We see them do this every day; but if it were proposed that the state should interfere, few would be led astray by the proposition.

The same principle applies to trade directly and completely. The productive powers of men and communities differ, but whatever they are, more or less, they reach their maximum under liberty. The total of national wealth is greatest where each disposes of his own energy in production and exchange with the least interference. This is not saying that none will make mistakes, or that free trade will eliminate all ills from human life. Free trade will not make the idle enjoy the fruits of industry, nor the thriftless possess the rewards of economy. Poverty, pain, disease, misery will remain as long as idleness and vice remain. Free trade will only act in its own measure and way, to leave men face to face with these things, with a somewhat better chance to conquer them. It is one of the great vices of protection that it makes the industrious suffer for the idle, and the energetic and enterprising bear the losses of the stupid.

2. If, now, you examine the opposite theory you will find that it assumes that we or our ancestors all made a great mistake in coming to this country and trying to live here. We are told that a tariff is necessary to "make a market" for our farmers, that a tariff is necessary to keep our manufactures from destruction, that navigation laws are necessary to preserve our shipping. Some of the old countries support a population twenty or thirty times as dense as ours with little or nothing of this artificial system. If, then, we are not able to live here without this aid, we must have left a part of the world where life is easier for one where it is harder. This brings me, then,

3. To the great fundamental error of the theory, viz.: That taxation is a productive force. No emigrants go to the desert of Sahara. None would go to New York if it were sand and rocks. If, however, New York is a part of the earth's surface, consisting of arable land fit to produce food for man; if it is intersected by mountains, covered by forests, and containing iron and coal, and if it possesses great rivers and a splendid harbor, then the conditions of supporting human life are fulfilled. It requires only labor and capital to build up there a great and prosperous community. It is plain that some parts of the earth's surface contain more materials for man's use than others, and the fact as to New York will affect the wealth of its inhabitants. It is plain that it makes a difference whether the people are idle or industrious, listless or energetic, sluggish or enterprising. It is plain that it makes a difference how much capital they have, or whether there are enough of them for the best distribution of labor. It is plain that it makes a difference what is the state of the arts and sciences, and what are the facilities of transportation.

The wealth of New York at any given time must depend on the way in which these factors are combined. Now the question arises: How can taxation possibly increase the product? Which one of the factors does it act upon?

Just consider what taxation is. We pay taxes, in the first place, to pay for the necessary organization of society, in order that we may act together, and not at cross purposes like a mob; but if that were all the state had to do taxes would be very small. We must support courts and police, and army and navy. These we need for peace, and justice, and security. But suppose that there were none who had the will to rob, or to swindle, or to cheat, or to do violence, the expenditures under this head would dwindle to nothing. It follows that taxes are the tribute we pay to avarice, and violence, and rapine, and all the other vices which disfigure human nature. Taxes are only those evils translated into money and spread over the community. They are so much taken from the strength of the laborer, or the fertility of the soil, or the benefit of the climate. They are loss and waste to almost their entire extent.

This is the function of government, then, which it is proposed to use to create value, to do what men can do only by applying labor and capital to land. Let us take a case to test it. Let us suppose that no woolen cloth is made in New York, but that a New York farmer, at the end of a certain time, has ten bushels of wheat, of which one bushel will buy a yard of imported cloth. After the exchange then he has nine bushels of wheat and one yard of cloth. If any one could make cloth in New York as easily as he could raise a bushel of wheat, some one would do it as soon as there was unemployed labor and capital, and that would be the end of the matter; but if no one undertakes the business it must be because labor and capital are all employed, or because it takes more labor and capital to produce a yard of cloth than a bushel of wheat. Let us suppose that it would take as much as a bushel and a half of wheat. Now, a protectionist proposes to the state to tax imported cloth one-half bushel of wheat per yard. If his plan is carried out the difficulty of obtaining imported cloth is raised to one bushel and a half of wheat per yard, which is the rate of difficulty at which it can be produced in New York. The protectionist then begins and offers his cloth at a bushel and a half per yard. The farmer who, as before, has produced ten bushels, now buys at the new rate, and after the exchange stands possessed of eight and a half bushels of wheat and one yard of cloth. Whither has the other half bushel gone? It has gone to make up a fund to hire some men to make life in New York harder than God and nature made it. From time to time we are told how much "our industries have increased." So far as their increase is in fact due to this arrangement, it is only a proof how much mischief has been done. This application of taxation does not alter the nature of taxation, it only extends its effects arbitrarily and needlessly, and inflicts upon the people a greater measure than they need otherwise bear of the burden which is due to robbery, injustice, war, famine and the other social ills.

4. Protection is, moreover, hostile to improvements. We are always eager to devise improved methods and to invent machinery to "save labor," but every such improvement which we introduce involves the waste and destruction of a great deal of capital. Old machinery must be discarded, although it is not worn out. This loss is not incurred by anybody willingly; it is enforced by competition. When, therefore, competition is withdrawn or limited the incentive to improvement is lessened or destroyed. This applies especially in manufactures where the interna-

tional competition is cut off by protective duties. The same principle that protection resists improvement applies even more distinctly to those improvements which are made in transportation. In spite of their theories men rejoice in all the improved means of communication which bring nations nearer together. A new railroad or an improved steamship is regarded as a step gained in civilization. Such improvements are realized in diminished freights and diminished prices of imported goods. No sooner is this realized, however, than "foreign competition" is found to be worse than ever. An outcry goes up for "more protection," and a new tax is put on to-day to counteract what we rejoiced over yesterday as an immense gain. We spend millions to dredge out our harbors, to remove rocks and cut channels through sandbars, as if it were a gain to have communication inward and outward as free as possible, and as soon as we experience the effects in reduced cost of goods we lay a new tax, like restoring the sandbars, in order to undo our work. Indeed, to build sandbars across our harbors would be a far cheaper means of reaching the same end. Next, we find that the numerous and complicated taxes have made it impossible for us to build ships to sail across the ocean where they must come in competition with foreign ships; so we make navigation acts and forbid the purchase of ships, exclude foreigners from our coasting trade, and finally, propose bounties and subsidies, all of which must come at last out of the products of our labor, in order to try to get ships once more. It is like the man who cut a piece from his coat to mend his trowsers, a piece from his vest to replace the hole in his coat, a piece from his trowsers to restore his vest, and so on over again. Did he ever get a whole suit? He found in a little while that he had only a rag left.

We are told, however, that if we do not do all this we shall be "inundated" with foreign goods. The word is appalling, and carries with it a fallacy which often seems to have great power. On what terms shall we get this flood of good things? Will they be given to us? If so, what can we do better than to stop work and live on this generosity? Why are we, however, selected as the especial objects of this bounty, if bounty it is? Why do not England and France and Belgium and Germany pour out their inundations on Patagonia and Iceland? The answer is plain enough. The goods are not gifts, they are offered for exchange. Nothing can force us to buy or dictate terms of exchange; and the inundation comes to us because we are known to be rich and able, and because we inhabit a continent prolific in some of the chief objects of human desire. It is not the beggar who, when he goes down the street, is "inundated" with wares from the various stores. If it were he would probably stem the tide with joy. It is the rich man only to whom good things are freely offered with a well understood condition; few rich men have ever been heard to complain of it. If, then, the Americans have these good things offered them in exchange and they allow themselves to be worsted in the bargain, they sadly belie their reputation.

These few observations which I have now presented as bearing on this subject are very broad and comprehensive, and very sweeping in their effect. They appeal directly to common sense and right reason. They give us the correct point of view, and dispel some of the fog which has collected from habit and prejudice around this subject. They lead us right up to the doctrine which the United States have put in practice in their own internal trade—absolute freedom of exchange and local or internal taxation. We have proved the practical value of that system here over a continent. I cannot see why the same system would not be a great gain if extended over Canada, Mexico and the West Indies. I cannot see why it would not be a great gain if all South America were embraced in a confederation exactly like ours as far as this point is concerned, with absolute free trade between the states. I cannot see why all Europe would not gain by similar relations, as far as trade is concerned; and I see no reason why it should not be equally beneficent if extended to the whole civilized globe.

The objections come in the shape of stubborn prejudices and old errors attaching to narrow and special considerations. Some people dread the sweep of a great general principle, however clear and certain and scientific it may be. They dispose of it as a "theory." Well, I am a theorist. I accept the disabilities and demand the advantages of my position; and when I find a great principle founded in an observation of facts and experience, I am not afraid to follow it up to its last corollary. The statesman must do what he can in the face of tradition and prejudice and vested interests, and I presume that it will be long before the public will be so enlightened as to demand to feel every cent that it pays in taxes for the very sake of knowing the amount, but I am clear in regard to the wisdom of such an arrangement.

In the further lectures which I am to give I propose to treat the subject historically for I believe that the tariff history of the United States shows most clearly some of the worst of the evils of the system, and I think that every one ought to know how this system has grown up and been fastened upon us.

LECTURE III

THE ORIGIN OF PROTECTION IN THIS COUNTRY.

The war of American Independence was a revolt against unjust taxation. In the same year the Declaration of Independence was adopted, and Adam Smith published his "Wealth of Nations." They were two revolts, one political, the other scientific, against the prevailing dogmas of the mercantile system of political economy. They were twin incidents in the revolt of modern life against the traditions of the middle age. It is at once a pity and a surprise that the last century has seen their developments diverge instead of combining.

The revolt of the American colonies was against the "colonial system," which was itself only a part of a grand theory about the relations of nations as regards trade. According to this theory, nations were to be isolated from each other. They were not regarded as merely groups in the body of mankind, having common interests, but as distinct and separate bodies, having hostile interests, and ruled in their relations to one another by jealousy, suspicion and desire for plunder. Civilization had advanced so far that these motives were regarded inside the nation as barbarous and injurious, but they still prevailed in international relations. In regard to trade, it was believed that its object was to get possession of money—precious metals—that this was wealth, and that only one party to an exchange could gain by it. It naturally followed that complicated laws were made to control trade and drive it into the forms which men thought wiser and better than those of nature. Export duties were laid on raw materials to make them cheap; bounties were laid on exports of manufactured goods in order to increase exports; duties were laid on imports to diminish them; prohibitions were laid on the exportation of specie, or on the exportation of machinery, or on the emigration of laborers. Navigation laws, including discriminating duties and tonnage taxes were passed. All this belonged to the great system: the effect was to isolate nations, to rob them of each other's gains in literature and the arts and sciences, and to cut off all that highest development which comes from the action of states on states.

When this system was complete and the barriers were established, nations began to put in special gates, well defended, at which they agreed to let each other in and out for special forms of trade, at particular times and under strict regulations. We ask, in astonishment, if this was trade;

if men really believed that trade must be watched and restrained in this way. We see that the private trader cannot make his place of business too attractive, nor set the door too wide open, nor make the approach too easy, nor be too indifferent as to who comes, or how, provided he comes for honest trade. But the method we here find in use suggests only dread, suspicion and war. The machinery is that of a fortress, not that of a market.

The colonial system was only a part of this system. When the old States had all been thus isolated they began to seek possessions in the new world, with which each for itself could hold free trade but exclude all others. That is, foreign commerce was, after all, a good thing, and free trade was a good thing, if you could hold the foreign nation in subjection and coerce all its relations. If the colony could be used for the interest of the mother country, freedom, on this theory, became a good thing for trade. This theory had an obvious weakness, that if the colony ever got strong enough it would not endure this warping of all its energies in one direction, but would get independence in order to come into free relations with other nations besides its mother country. Such is the actual meaning of the American war of independence.

It would seem natural that the emancipated colonies would seek *free* intercourse with all nations, and it is a very curious study to see how this logical tendency conflicted for years after the revolution with inherited traditions and prejudices. On the 6th February, 1778, Gerard, Franklin, Deane and Lee made a treaty of alliance and also a treaty of commerce between France and the United States. In the latter treaty it was agreed to avoid "all those burthensome prejudices which are usually sources of debate, embarrassment and discontent," and to take as the "basis of their agreement the most perfect equality and reciprocity.' They further refer to the general principle by which they were guided as that of "founding the advantage of commerce solely upon reciprocal utility and the just rules of free intercourse." Up to this time the principle of treaties of commerce had been that two nations made an agreement to give each other special and exclusive privileges. The Americans introduced this much of a new principle, that they would not enter into those complicated relations by which Europe, after having cut off all natural relations, had set up special, narrow, arbitrary and artificial relations between nations, but that they would hold themselves open to the freest relations they could establish with all parts of the old world.

Hence we find their representatives abroad eagerly pushing, at every opportunity, for chances to establish commercial relations. They met with all kinds of obstacles. Old habit had accustomed nations to deal with their own colonies only. They had no idea what good things the North American colonies could offer. The habit of suspicion was strong.

and the prevailing notions of trade led them to apprehend dangers rather than advantages from trade. On the other hand, as it had generally been believed that England had gained great advantages from her colonies, there was great eagerness to get a share in those advantages now that they were free and open, if only the aspirants had been able to find out what those advantages were and how to obtain them.

It is strange to read the correspondence of the American agents abroad, and to see how they argued and discussed with grave ambassadors about the "loss" which one nation would suffer in trading with another, any shipment of specie one way or the other being regarded as an infallible sign of loss. The Americans were by no means clear in their ideas, and did not combat these notions on principle, but apparently coincided in them. They sought equality and reciprocity, but they never rose to the height of the only true doctrine. In an exchange both parties win, or else obviously one would refuse to trade. If then one party puts obstacles in the way, the total gain is diminished, the diminution probably being divided. If the other party creates an obstacle, the gain is still further diminished or destroyed. It is a matter of regret therefore when one party is guilty of this folly, but it only doubles the mischief, and still further injures the other, if he likewise perpetrates the same folly. This is the answer to the well worn and stubborn notion that free trade must be reciprocal, or would be good if all nations would adopt it. One nation which adopts free trade gets more than it would if it put on restraints, even though all other nations may have restraints. It will share the gain if they follow its example, for the gain is multiplied at every step, but, even while they hold back, it gains as much as it can and makes the best of a bad state of things, while waiting for them to come to a better mind, if it adopts freedom. What would be thought of a grocer who refused to trade with the hatter who would sell him the best hats at the lowest price, because the hatter did not buy flour and sugar of him?

The American ministers had little success in their efforts to make treaties such as I have described. The one with England was the one most eagerly desired. Under the prevailing notions the English had expected to suffer immense losses by the separation, but habit and the excellence of English goods revived trade immediately after the war, and the trade was found as good as ever. A treaty which would have been eagerly seized in 1782 was refused in 1785. They did not care for any treaty.

Here we come to the first case in which currency errors became intertwined with errors as to foreign trade, a junction which has run through all our history to the present moment and which has been proof of mischief. In 1781, after the downfall of the continental currency, specie became very abundant here, being bought by both French and English. The States, however, still had vast quantities of paper afloat. As soon as the war ended this specie was all exported and expended in the purchase of goods long missed. The export of specie in 1783 was ten millions. The import of goods from England in 1785 was 10 millions, and the exports 3.9 millions. In 1770 the imports were 8.5 millions, and the exports 4.5 millions. This explains why the English were so well satisfied with the revival of trade.

During the war many industries had sprung up to supply the wants of the people for manufactures formerly imported. At the return of peace these industries were prostrated, and a cry began to be made at that time that the country could not stand free trade, and that it must do as England had always done, that is, imitate the old restrictive system. The real demand was that some way should be found by law to continue upon the American people, by their own act, the evils which the war had inflicted on them. We shall see more of this when we come to the tariff of 1816. Whatever may have been the effect of peace to destroy the war mushrooms, we find that there were, in 1789, manufactures of iron, glass, paper and cloth here, which were boasted of as strong and prosperous, and propositions were made by competent capitalists for mining iron on a large scale in Pennsylvania, which fell only on account of the turbulency of the inhabitants and the insecurity of titles.

While things were in this state, Adams wrote from England in great disgust at the rejection of his treaty, and urged reprisals. He declared that we could get no treaty until we should set up restrictions, that is, we were to put a hindrance in the way in order to make a bargain for getting English obstacles removed by promising to remove ours. Massachusetts took this advice, but found that it drove trade away to Newport and Portsmouth. Virginia did the same, and found that she had likewise benefited Maryland and North Carolina.

Meanwhile the government of the Confederation was falling to pieces, and was a pity and a laughing stock. It had no revenues and could not pay instalments on its loans as they fell due, nor even the interest on its debt. Misery was great throughout the country, owing to paper money and debt and the losses of war. The people were discontented and rebellious, actual disorder occurring in Massachusetts, Pennsylvania and North Carolina. The Congress was begging the States to lay a uniform five per cent. duty to provide a revenue for the Confederation. The question of import tax was, therefore, bound up with the question of civil order, protection to manufactures, foreign commercial relations, and the misery arising from bad currency at home. Virginia having tried to come to an agreement with Maryland to enforce a common revenue system on the great waters of those States, this was found to be impracticable without the coöperation of other States. This led to the Congress of Annapolis in 1786, which was only a commercial convention, and which found no better way to discharge the task it had undertaken than to recommend Congress to call another convention in the following year to revise the Articles of Confederation; that is, to provide for a common revenue system, and for "the regulation of commerce," by giving the general government permanent power for those purposes. The Convention, when it met, made a complete reconstruction of the Articles of Confederation and gave us the present Constitution. You see, then, just how much truth there is in the assertion that the country was ruined by free trade during the Confederation, and that the Constitution was made to give protection.

In the Constitutional Convention, the question of free trade came up under the form of a desire for a navigation law, and it at once took a sectional form. The Eastern States wanted the Constitution chiefly in order to get such a law. The Southernmost States wanted free trade. The positions of the two sections were inverted in regard to slavery, while some of the Middle States wanted neither navigation laws nor slavery. It was one of the compromises of the Constitution that the power to regulate commerce was inserted, together with the allowance of the slave trade until 1808 (under the permission to tax slaves not over ten dollars per head), and the prohibition of export duties.

No sooner did the House of Representatives get a quorum than the subject of revenue came up, and no sooner was the subject of revenue taken up than the question of protection was raised.

In the debate, Madison said:

"I own myself the friend of a very free system of commerce. If industry and labor are left to take their own course they will generally be directed to those objects which are most productive, and that in a manner more certain and direct than the wisdom of the most enlightened legislature could point out. Nor do I believe that the national interest is more promoted by such legislative directions than the interest of the individuals concerned. Yet I concede that exceptions exist to this general rule, important in themselves, and claiming the particular attention of this committee. If America were to leave her ports perfectly free, and to make no discrimination between vessels owned by citizens and those owned by foreigners, while other nations make such discrimination, such a policy would go to exclude American shipping from foreign ports, and we should be materially affected in one of our most important interests."

Again, in reply to Fitzsimmons, of Pennsylvania, who wanted more protection, and wanted to discourage luxury, and made certain propositions to that end, he said: "Some of the propositions may be productive of revenue, and some may protect our domestic manufactures, though the latter subject, which involves some intricate questions, ought not to be too confusedly blended with the former."

That is to say, he was one of those who believe that a doctrine can be true and its application unwise, and he thought that the coercion to be exercised on somebody else by doing one's self an injury was sufficient cause for submitting to suffering. He also tried very hard, on this and subsequent occasions, but fortunately in vain, to introduce discriminating duties as between the nations with which we had treaties and those with which we had none.

Perhaps the most remarkable utterance which has ever been made in the discussion of this tariff question was made by Fisher Ames in this debate of 1789. He said: "From the different situation of the manufacturers in Europe and America, encouragement is necessary. In Europe the artisan is driven to labor for his bread. Stern necessity, with her iron rod, compels his exertion. In America, invitation and encouragement are needed. Without them the infant manufacture droops, and those who might be employed in it seek with success a competency from our cheap and fertile soil." For a man to adduce the facts which are the grandest argument on one side of the question as an argument on the other is not common, and that a man like Fisher Ames could do it is a proof of the depth to which long rooted notions can affect a man's mind. The argument amounts to saying that it is so easy for laborers to get a living in America, that we must make it hard to get a living here in order that work may be done. It states the protectionist position in America, however, with great exactness. The cheap and fertile soil, by nature, holds out to men of the artisan class a competency in return for moderate and easy labor. In order that they might be forced to work at manufactures, which were, in the nature of things, less remunerative in a new country with boundless fertile soil, it was necessary to curtail by artificial and legal arrangements the profits of agriculture. This is just what the tariff has done from 1789 until this day. We are more familiar with the argument under the form of the comparative rates of wages here and abroad, but it comes back to just what Ames so simply stated. The competition which the protectionist employer has had to contend against here has never been the cheapness of foreign labor; it has been the greater return which his men could get by putting the same labor on the soil. That is the only meaning of the high wages in this country. What makes wages high? Where do they come from? Or why is it that artisans are told that protection makes wages high? How are these things reconcilable? Or how is it that the foreign labor with which we are told that we cannot compete is especially that of England, where wages are higher than anywhere else in Europe? Or why is it that high-priced labor can compete here in agriculture and stand three or four thousand miles of transportation ? Wages are high here because men of the wages class can get all the fertile land they can till by going to it; because the capital required is very small, and because the returns are almost pure reward of labor. Hence they will not go into the wages class unless the inducement is equal. It is the great form in which the new country holds out grand opportunities to the man who has nothing but his manual labor to depend upon, and the protective system does, and always has taken away from the farmer, laborer and artisan, the advantages which nature offered him in the new country.

To return to the tariff debate of 1789. The character of all tariff legislation in this country, as a grand grab struggle between interests and sections, was illustrated then.

The South, except Georgia, wanted a high tariff duty on rum, for revenue; the Middle States, in the interest of temperance, the Eastern States, for protection to their rum distilleries. Georgia opposed this tax because she used a great deal of rum, and bought it in the West Indies with her lumber. The Southern and Middle States wanted a tax also on molasses, but this the Eastern States vigorously opposed. Molasses was the raw material of rum. It was bought with salt fish, lumber and staves sent to the West Indies. Rum was itself an export to Africa. Both the Eastern States, in this case, and Georgia, in the preceding, felt and urged the truth which the South urged in 1832, but which the manufacturers scouted, that the tariff on imports would diminish the trade and lessen the exports; that is, cripple the "home industry." Our present tariff is unquestionably acting in the same way on all the great staple agricultural industries of the country which export their product.

The South opposed the tax on iron and steel, as all agricultural interests must. The Pennsylvanians replied that the manufacture was already established in their State, and that a slight duty would, "in a little while," lead to a great production.

The South wanted a protective tax on hemp, claiming that rice and indigo were unprofitable. Pennsylvania opposed any tax on hemp as a raw material of cordage, but wanted a tax on that. New England opposed the tax on cordage as a raw material of ships, but wanted protection on the latter. In the midst of this wrangling effort to invent some way by law to enable people to get rich in the country, it is interesting to notice that cotton was only incidentally alluded to. A tax of three cents a pound was put upon it, on the chances that it might come to something. This well illustrates the amount of foresight that statesmen can ever exercise in these matters. They passed over an article, destined by natural circumstances to become one of the great staples of the country, while they were looking for something to encourage, and when they found such an article, whose value lay in nature and fact, it was totally beyond their puny systems of artificial aid.

The South opposed any duty on spikes or nails. Goodhue replied for New England, that they were already exported, and that a tax would soon produce enough for all North America. It was a "domestic manufacture" in chimney corners. "Domestic manufactures" was a term then used for household manufactures, which were regarded with great favor as a desirable thing.

For twenty-five years after this time protectionist journals gathered instances of farmers whose wives or daughters spun and wove, and whose sons spent the evening in making nails at the chimney corner, and such journals paraded these cases as glorious instances of industry. This went on long after machinery had so cheapened these manufactures that an hour's farm work would pay for more goods of this kind than people could make by hand in a day, but the old people who clung to the method were pointed to as models, and the young people who preferred printed calicoes to homespun and leisure to nail-making, were scolded for their extravagance. This opinion had no necessary connection with protection, but it sprang from the general erroneous point of view that we want work for the sake of work, and not for the sake of results; that industry is a good thing, not because it produces more goods, but because it is work; that the ideal of life is not abundance with leisure, but scarcity with toil. Hence it seems wise to refuse the benefits of machinery owned by foreigners in the first place, and before they know it, those who advocate protection to bring factories into being are applauding those who refuse to profit by the machinery when established.

New England and Virginia, which latter then expected to become a ship-building State, favored navigation acts as protection to shipping. The other States, as freight-payers and not ship owners, objected. A discriminating tonnage duty was laid, and ten per cent. was reduced from duties on goods imported in American ships. A special discriminating duty was laid on tea, because the tea trade could only be carried on by "a drain of specie." The wars in Europe and the increased trade of neutrals during the next twenty-five years led to an immense increase of American shipping independent of protection, but it became an important precedent, as I shall show, in the tariff debate of 1816.

The tariff of 1789 avowedly adopted the principle of protection. The preamble read as follows: "Whereas, it is necessary for the support of the Government, for the discharge of the debts of the United States, and the encouragement and protection of manufactures, that duties be laid, &c." It was declared to be only temporary in order to give infant industries a start, and was limited to 1796. The duties levied under it were equivalent to an *ad valorem* rate of $8\frac{1}{2}$ per cent. During the debate some fears were expressed that the duties might be so high as to encourage smuggling. To this Mr. Madison replied that he "would not believe that the virtue of our citizens was so weak as not to resist that temptation to smuggling which a seeming interest might create. Their conduct under the British Government was no proof of a disposition to evade a just tax. At that time they conceived themselves oppressed by a nation in whose councils they had no share, and on that principle resistance was justified to their consciences. The case was now altered; all had a voice in every regulation, and he did not despair of a great revolution in sentiment when it came to be understood that the man who wounds the honor of his country by a baseness in defrauding the revenue, at the same time exposes his neighbors to further impositions."

This tariff, then, was the thin edge of the wedge. The duties were raised the next year so as to equal an 11 per cent. *ad valorem* rate, and in 1792 they were raised to equal 13½ per cent. Between the tariff of 1789 and that of 1816, a period of twenty-six years, seventeen acts were passed affecting duties, generally and steadily raising them.

The most important incident in this early tariff history was Hamilton's report on the manufactures, December 5, 1791. It came from a man who held and deserved high authority as a statesman, and it dealt with the subject in a comprehensive manner. It has been the arsenal from which our popular school of protectionists have borrowed ever since. Its political economy, however, is very erroneous, and defective in many fundamental respects. It is erroneous as to wages, and it confuses credit, capital and money. It is marked throughout by the errors of the old mercantile system, hinging all its views of foreign trade on the import or export of specie to be occasioned. Thus Hamilton says: "The West India Islands, the soils of which are the most fertile, and the nation which in the greatest degree supplies the rest of the world with the precious metals, exchange to a loss with almost every other country."

He admits the force of the broad free trade arguments, but thinks that while other nations follow the restrictive system, the United States must do so. He speaks of the hindrances met with in attempting to export American products, which would seem to point to a general conviction of the mischief of the entire restrictive system, and not to the conclusion that the United States ought to adopt the same policy. Though led to advocate protection on this special plea, he goes on to try to give it a theoretical justification. We shall have occasion to notice this again; but I beg you here to observe the difference. If the argument was made, as it often was for our first half century, that free trade was good, but that we must restrict because others did, it would follow that we ought to abandon restriction as fast and as far as others did. If the argument was based on principle and theory, it would be good any time.

for all nations, and forever. The argument of expediency was used, however, as in this report of Hamilton, to break the force of the common sense free trade view, and the theoretical argument was smuggled in behind it. He distinguishes seven particulars in which he thinks protection is theoretically advantageous. Of these, three, "the division of labor," "affording greater scope for the diversity of talents," and "affording a more ample and various field for enterprise," are only subdivisions of the great doctrine of the "diversification of industry," and may be noticed under that head. The issue here between the free trader and the protectionist depends on radically different views of human society. The question is whether industry diversifies itself as chances arise under the operation of natural forces, so that man can neither hasten the process nor retard it without doing injury; or whether the legislature must be always on the watch to discharge a heavy responsibility resting upon it, viz., to tell society when and how to adjust itself into groups for industrial purposes. The industrial history of the American colonies offers the best proof in the world of the truth of the former view. There we see communities growing from the simplest germ, isolated to a certain extent. We see that the development of society is as regular and as natural as that of a plant, and there is no more need of human interference than there is to make a bud burst into a blossom at the proper moment. It is a development, moreover, which cannot be hastened without injury. A new country cannot have the higher social developments until its population begins to grow dense. It is so with us yet. We have not the literature or the science or the fine arts of the old countries, but we have not their poverty and misery. We must take our advantages and disadvantages together.

Now the diversification of industry comes, so far as it is desirable or advantageous, of itself. We must wait for it till it comes, and we must take it when it comes. The South will find its interest in cotton culture as a great prevailing industry for a long time to come. The same is true of the wheat of the West. No preaching can induce men to abandon the industry which is the most lucrative, and no law can make them do it without injuring their interest. As for the scope for varied talents, persons go to the places which offer an arena for their talents. They do not sit still and say: "Let us make an arena here." The tendency of man, as transportation is made easier and emigration freer, is to stop trying to coerce nature, and to put himself where nature spontaneously aids him. As for the division of labor, it is just as great and just as advantageous, now that transportation is easy, if the laborers are locally distributed as if they are industrially distributed. Look at the distribution in our own country. The South raises raw materials, the West raises food, and the East manufactures. As for the varied field of enterprise, the world opens that, and our enterprises seek the place of advantage.

Hamilton next says that protection extends the use of machinery. He means that if there are manufactures, there is more use for machinery than there is in agriculture. On this view you do the business to use the machinery, you do not use machinery to do the business.

Next he argues that protection furnishes additional employment to classes not formerly engaged in the business. This is the argument that protection makes work. It is very true that protection makes work, but that it makes more work without making more product. It increases the human exertion necessary to gain the same amount of good.

He had in view domestic work auxiliary to adjacent manufactories. He thinks that the factories offer employment to the wives and children of farmers, in work which they can do at home. He refers to the children employed in factories in England, and he thinks that the farmer's income might be enlarged by this aid. Let us realize the facts. An American farmer could, by virtue of the advantages of the new country, if untrammeled by interference, support himself and a family by his own labor. Farm work furnishes opportunity for the participation of all the family to a certain degree. Beyond that the farmer could give his wife leisure for the culture and accomplishments of life. He could also support his children up to maturity, giving them a long and complete education. Now adopt the protective system and put up a fostered industry by the side of his farm. I think it very likely that you would soon find his wife spending her time over work from the factory, and his children curtailed of their time of education and sent to work in it. It would be found necessary to take some such step to keep up the family income to the old figure. Work would be made for the wife and children, and the amount of that work which they would be obliged to do would be no unfair measure of the harm the restrictive system had inflicted on the farmer. The protective system simply lowers the social attainments of farmers and farmers' wives, and lessens the degree of education to which farmers' children can aspire.

The next object which Hamilton thought that a protective system could attain was the promotion of immigration. The best examination of this claim is to look at the fact as to what immigration has taken place. Of course protection cannot be credited with any other immigration than that which has taken place amongst workmen in the protected industries. The total immigration for fifty-one years, from 1820 to 1870, was 7,800,000. Of these 4,800,000, or 61 per cent., had no occupation or stated none. They were mostly women and children and laborers, supplying manual labor, which the new country demanded in large quantities. The next largest number was of laborers so reported, 1,300,000.

The next number was of farmers, 900,000, bearing witness to the attractions of the natural advantages of the country simply. The next number was of mechanics, not specified, 500,000. Of the others, the only ones possibly included in protected industries were, miners, 92,181; weavers and spinners, 14,790 (of whom nearly half came between 1830 and 1840, when, as is well known, large numbers of persons in these trades came from England on account of the introduction of machinery, and sought other employment here); manufacturers, 4,520. Now, if we look at the half million mechanics, we find that very few of them belong to industries which are protected. For the sake of a closer examination, take a year of high protection and very large immigration, 1870. The total immigration was 387,203. Of these, those classified as "skilled workmen," numbered 31,964. Of these, 8,061 were "mechanics not stated," leaving say 24,000. The largest numbers amongst these were, blacksmiths, 2,378; carpenters, 4,421; masons, 2,190; shoemakers, 1,557; tailors, 1,660 (none of whom certainly profited by protection); miners, 4,763; weavers, 1,178 (who came into more or less protection). The others who belonged to protected industries were, brewers, 362; cutlers, 5; distillers, 2; file-makers, 2; gunsmiths, 2; hatters, 58; hoemaker, 1; instrument maker, 1; iron workers, 3; jewelers, 409; nailmakers, 19; potters, 8; printers, 180; puddlers, 2; rope-makers, 3; saddlers, 167; shipwrights, 9; soap-makers, 2; spinners, 7; tanners, 102; wool-sorter, 1; operatives, 23; shepherds, 23. Out of a total of 387,203 immigrants, the number who came to make articles which either could be or were protected was 6,960, or less than two per cent. It appears that protection has not drawn immigrants, as a matter of fact.

Hamilton's next point is that protection secures a more certain and steady market for the products of the soil. This is the notion of the "home market." Hamilton urged it on the ground that foreign restrictions hindered the exportation of an agricultural surplus. He thought it necessary for government to take the matter in hand and provide or secure a home market. Obviously it is an advantage to any new country to increase its inhabitants. If such increase took place anywhere there must follow an increased production.

Now, for the sake of brevity, I will state in general terms what happens, although every proposition might be illustrated abundantly from our own colonial history. The industries which begin first in a new country are those which the economists call "extractive industries." They require little capital, and admit of little division of labor. They are agriculture, lumbering, hunting or trapping, fishing and mining. Some mechanics are needed in the building trades. In regard to these persons, one principle I have already stated was illustrated in the early history of Massachusetts. They would not work except at wages which would equal the remuneration which they could get in the industries mentioned. The way the Puritans tried to deal with the problem was to fix wages by law, but the men either took to agriculture, or went on to other settlements where there was no such law. At first, every farmer is his own wheelwright and blacksmith and carpenter. As the population increases there is a surplus of agricultural products. Some who have greater skill or taste for the mechanical arts work in those occupations for others until the division of labor becomes established gradually and naturally. Some products are exported, being raw materials of great demand. Manufactured goods, cloth, tools, books, paper, and all the comforts and conveniences of the old life of the colonists are imported in exchange. Some become merchants to carry on this exchange, and build a town at the seaport. At first, clergymen and schoolmasters may be the only professional men, and they act as lawyers and doctors. All participate in legislation; merchants do all the banking. As the population increases and the country fills up the extractive industries become less lucrative. The sources for some of them become exhausted, the supplies of others become superabundant. Farming itself undergoes subdivisions and refinements. Orchards are planted for fruit, and gardens for vegetables. Stock raising becomes profitable, and dairy farming is extended. Simultaneously with this, without any dividing line, or any exertion whatever, the simple mechanic arts which existed at the outset grow into independent manufactures, according to the circumstances of the case. It depends on the distance of the colony, the facility of transportation, the market for its surplus abroad, the amount of land open, how soon or how rapidly this social organization will be developed. If foreign nations all had severe restrictions upon the entrance of the goods this country wanted to export, they would put just so much premium on the early development of manufactures there. The whole tendency of a surplus supply of food would be to force some of the producers of it to seek some other employment, in which they would produce other things to exchange with their neighbors for food. Every refusal of a foreign country to take the only things the new country could offer in exchange for its goods would throw the inhabitants back on their neighbors to supply the want by such exchange. Every such act would, moreover, diminish the value of the surplus, that is, would increase the amount which the farmer could afford to give his neighbor for making his cloth and iron for him. The "home market" would thus "provide" itself, if it was wanted, and the want itself would be the result of foreign errors, injuring in just so far the community in question. If one of their own statesmen took it into his head that it was his business to provide a home market, he could only do it by adopting the restrictive system, and still further depressing the profits of agriculture, and thus accelerating the mischievous process already at work.

The repeal of the corn laws in England was accordingly a great blow to American manufactures, because it allowed American agriculture to come to a part of its natural rights, and we have been trying, ever since 1861, to neutralize this by heavier pressure of taxation. That same repeal, however, took away all Hamilton's argument, and the general argument has since been altered. We have been told lately that protection is to bring the manufacturer and the farmer near together; to give the farmer a market near his own door, and in various ways the export of agricultural produce has been represented as an evil. But when we talk of "bringing" the manufacturer and farmer together, it may fairly be asked: Who is to "bring?" This is language for an Assyrian king, deporting inhabitants from one part of a country to another. If the manufacturer finds the conditions of successful industry lead him to a certain spot, well and good. That spot will enjoy the benefit of its peculiar advantages. But if it has no such advantages, and we plant a factory there, shall we thereby give them to it? Shall we ever get back the expended force? Shall we not rather suffer loss so long as the artificial creation stands where it ought not to be? Will not that loss come out of the legitimate, sound and healthy industries? The error is in thinking that we ever can get out of an artificial creation any more than we put into it; it is only when we get nature to work with us and for us, that we can get anything gratuitously. The American farmer has long ago found that there cannot be two prices in the same market; that he does not get any different price for his wheat if consumed next door from that which he gets if it is consumed in Manchester. He rarely knows where it is consumed and never cares.

The whole idea of advantage in bringing farmer and manufacturer together is a delusion. It is much more important to bring the various manufacturers together, because they form groups which assist and sustain each other, and it is important to bring them to the country or place where the conditions of success exist. This place will not be where the profits of capital and the wages of labor in either agriculture or commerce are exceptionally high. Hence to carry a factory by force into an agricultural district will be to ruin the factory and not help the farmer. Where the profits of one industry far exceed those of all others, we have that one only. Where the profits of several are equal, we have them all. The advantages and disadvantages of either state of things are about equal.

Hamilton next proceeds to consider the objection to manufactures, that they are impossible here on account of the dearness of labor and the scarcity of capital. He reduces both these objections to a minimum, but shows thereby that protection was not necessary, and proves finally that manufactures were possible by enumerating many which were already thriving. In fact the country became very prosperous in 1789 and 1790 so soon as civil order was secured.

Further on again he urges an argument which is especially interesting because at a later time it became very popular: that protection lowers prices through the home competition. One is impelled to ask why, then, those interested desire it. Who would urge Government interference to lower the price of his goods? If the Government should so act, who would not cry out to be "let alone"? Nevertheless, the assertion is not without truth, only it is not all the truth. The first effect of a tariff is to draw many persons into the protected industries who believe that the tariff gives them full margin, and that special knowledge, or business care, or sagacity in choice of situation are not necessary. Factories are built extravagantly, or in bad situations. There follows large production, a glut, a fall in prices, perhaps even below foreign prices. Then come failures of those who have been most reckless. Then the remaining strong firms continue and adopt rules to "limit production," the necessary manipulation of any monopoly. Prices rise again on a limited supply, and the operation is repeated unless the combination is really strong enough to keep others out. These fluctuations are the real character of a tariff system, not either high prices or low prices, and they are one great reason why protection does not protect.

Hamilton next considers the means of protection, of which he enumerates eleven. These are import duties, prohibition on imports, prohibitions on exports, bounties, premiums, drawbacks, patents, inspection laws, facilitation of remittances, and improvements in transportation.

It is worth while to notice and pay tribute to the good faith of this statesman, who, however mistaken, believed that he was working for his country's good. He was not an advocate of a special interest, and he, at any rate, treated his subject philosophically. You have here the whole system of interference logically carried out. Bounties, patents, premiums, inspection laws, Government banking, and subsidies to transportation— all belong to one consistent theory, and you are dealing with a man who, at any rate, could seize a principle and either pursue it as true or abandon it as false. The issue comes squarely before you. Either it is the business of Government to do all these things or none. You either want a paternal Government or you want a Government which is merely a reserved force in behalf of peace, justice and security, and which is at its best when it has the least occasion to act. Hamilton's scheme has been very unequally carried out. Export duties are forbidden in the Constitution. Bounties on exports we have never directly employed. Drawbacks are substantially the same thing, although they are professedly intended to counterbalance duties on raw materials. Direct bounties and premiums we have not used, because the loss would be too distinctly seen. For that reason, however, they would be the best arrangement of all if we were to go into the system at all. By the census of 1870, the laborers engaged in manufacturing pig-iron numbered altogether 27,554, and their wages amounted to $12,400,000. The capital employed is returned at $56,100,000. We are pointed to this as a great industry—a grand thing to have. The duty was, when the census was taken, $9 per ton, and the market price of American over imported iron showed that this sum was directly added to the cost of all we used. The product of the home manufacture was 2,000,000 tons, on which the tariff cost us $18,000,000, of which the public treasury got not one cent. Seven per cent. on the capital in pig-iron manufacture would be $3,900,000, which, with the wages paid to laborers in that trade, would make $16,000,000. If, therefore, we had made a bargain with the pig-iron manufacturers to let their capital decay, paying them seven per cent. on it, and with the people employed to stay idle while we paid them their full wages, provided that we might have our iron free, we should have made $2,000,000 per annum, to say nothing of the fact that, at the lower price, we might have afforded a much larger consumption of iron. We should, moreover, have had 509 steam engines to apply to other work. We should have saved $18,000,000 worth of coal, charcoal and coke for other uses, and we should have left 4,000,000 tons of iron ore in the ground for those who come after us to use when they can do it profitably. All this is on the protectionist hypothesis that this industry would not have existed but for the tariff, a hypothesis which I by no means admit. Now, if we had had a bounty on iron, instead of a tariff, these facts would be far more generally known than they are. Inspection laws have been gradually laid aside, because they interfere with trade. They are ostensibly in the public interest, and far less objectionable than the other means mentioned; but here the cry has been raised to be "let alone." Patents we have extended more and more, until any plea which may be made for them is overwhelmed under their abuse. The other devices, Government banking and subsidies, we are still struggling with.

I have spent so much time and attention on this paper of Hamilton, because it has been historically of very great importance. It is the best statement of the protectionist argument ever made, and demands this much attention in any general discussion of the question. In the ten years following its preparation, during which Hamilton, either directly or indirectly, controlled the financial policy of the Government, it was found necessary to raise greater and greater revenue. Hamilton had, in presenting his plan, been very careful to define the limits within which he thought that the means he proposed might be safely and wisely employed. In his further financial steps he by no means extended and advanced the import duties with a view either to revenue or protection. He introduced internal and direct taxes for the avowed purpose of establishing a well balanced system of taxation. These taxes were all repealed on Jefferson's accession in 1802. Hamilton also prepared the system for assessing and collecting internal taxes which was revived in the second war with England, and again during the late war. Its reintroduction on each of these occasions took time, involved great delay and inconvenience, and caused expense which would have gone far to pay for keeping it up during the interval.

LECTURE IV.

THE ESTABLISHMENT OF PROTECTION IN THIS COUNTRY.

In my last lecture I sketched the origin of the protective system in this country. I now proceed to describe its growth and establishment. This was brought about by incidents connected with the Napoleonic wars. The wars of the French revolution, and those which followed, produced great effects upon the trade of the civilized world. The United States, as the chief neutral carrier, saw its shipping multiplied and its mercantile interests enriched. The belligerents, in their struggles to injure each other, endeavored to put a stop to this neutral traffic, and inflicted great injury on the neutral who was carrying it on. Nevertheless, the profits were so great that the Americans continued it, in spite of losses. When war broke out again in 1803, the indignation here at the collisions which took place was so great, that measures of resistance and retaliation were sought. The federalists wanted to put the country in a state of defence and build a navy to protect commerce. They represented the Northeastern States and the shipping interests. The administration, however, with the great majority from the Middle and Southern States, demanded a navy, sought to reduce expenditures, and turned its attention to measures of coercion by commercial war. These measures had been tried with sad results during the revolution. Mr. Madison had urged discriminating duties in the first tariff as a means of forcing foreign nations to grant reciprocity, and he had urged coercive and retaliatory measures of that kind during Washington's administration when hostilities in Europe first broke out. It is astonishing what faith was entertained in such measures. You see it still strong in the South when the civil war broke out, when it was believed that withholding cotton would force European nations to intervene.

In 1805 an act was passed for prohibiting the importation of English manufactures in order to force England to give up impressment, and in order to support Pinkney and Munroe in their efforts to make a treaty. In 1806 England blockaded the northern coast of Europe from Brest to the Elbe. Napoleon retaliated by the Berlin Decree. In the next year England replied by the orders in council; Napoleon rejoined by the Milan Decree, and England returned once more by more stringent prohibitions. The tenor of these decrees on the one side and on the other was to prohibit neutrals from trading with the enemy, or to put such trade under heavy restraints. Napoleon was trying to shut the continent against English manufactures, and England was trying to keep out of the continent provisions and colonial supplies. Between the two, neutral commerce suffered the greatest loss and vexation. The American shipowners complained and called on their government for protection. The measure adopted was the embargo of 1807, by which the shipowners were protected against foreign aggressors by being shut up at home. They had before incurred heavy risks, now their own government imposed certain ruin. It was necessary to pass one act after another, making the embargo more stringent and tyrannical in order to check evasions of it. It was repealed in a little over a year, but non-intercourse and non-importation acts were substituted for it until war grew out of it in 1812.

We are concerned with this commercial war here, not on account of its folly or imbecility, although it well represents the folly of all restriction, but on account of its connection with the strand of history which we are following. Embargo, non-intercourse, and war, lasting from 1807 to 1815, created an entirely artificial state of things here, or, perhaps I should say, the United States was drawn into the distortion and perversion of industry and commerce which the great wars were producing in Europe. Manufactories of various kinds sprang up here to supply the wants of the people when cut off from the usual sources of supply by foreign exchange. They produced articles of inferior quality or design, generally speaking, but people had to be satisfied with them. In many cases also the products were dearer than those normally obtainable abroad. They were sustained by the artificial difficulties in foreign exchange, and by the diminished profits of other industries which would have been more profitable here. In 1810, Gallatin, Secretary of the Treasury, made a report in which he stated that manufactures of wood and leather, amongst other things, were exported beyond the imports, that the following industries were "firmly established," iron and manufactures of iron, manufactures of cotton, wool and flax, paper, printing types, books, several manufactures of hemp, and a few others. In that year (1810) some effort was made to get more protection through duties, but nothing came of it. The same effort played some share in bringing about the war, which was a product of intrigue, and as needless as it was fruitless. One of the first war measures was to double all duties and prohibit the import of English products. During the war the prices of manufactured articles were very high. Manufacturers made great profits and factories were built in large numbers. In 1814 all the banks suspended specie payments, and then followed a reckless paper money period which has never been equalled since. Prices rose higher than ever, and here we have again an illustration of the observation previously made that our currency and tariff errors have been intertwined throughout our history.

Observe now the outcome of all this for the matter of our investigation. Embargo and war had created a false and artificial state of things in which much capital had been invested in manufactures, and "industry" had been "encouraged." Under the false light in which they were viewed, embargo and war, therefore, seemed to be beneficial forces. The return of peace, if it reopened trade and let things return to their normal condition, would be a calamity. It was necessary to secure a continuance of the circumstances which had brought these industries into existence, in order to secure them from destruction. Such continuance could not be brought about without perpetuating for the great body of consumers the scarcity, loss and distress of war, so far as war affected their power to procure and enjoy industrial products. This then is exactly what the tariff, which was adopted in 1816, did do. It saved a part of the capital involved in manufactures, although most of it was swept away in the financial crisis which ensued in 1819, on the collapse of the paper system, but it burdened the nation with the same trammels which embargo and war had laid upon it.

The act of May 3d, 1815, repealed all discriminating duties and tonnage taxes in favor of any nation which should take similar action with regard to American vessels and cargoes. Here we have a fact of interest to the general history which we are pursuing. This was what was known as the "American system," at this time. We saw how, in the treaty with France in 1778, the Americans set out to gain general reciprocity. That came to be called the "American system," viz., general reciprocity instead of the old commercial treaties. *Now* the plan of laying countervailing duties to enforce reciprocity came to be called the "American system," and was so called until 1824, when, by a still further perversion, that name was applied to the system of protective duties. Daniel Webster, at that time, well said of it: "This favorite American policy is what America has never tried; and this odious foreign policy is what, as we are told, foreign states have never pursued."

The act of February 5th, 1816, continued the double war duties until July 1, but the general tariff act was approved April 27th, 1816. The tariff was not at this time, or for sixteen years after, a political question, but it is noteworthy that tariffs were passed in every presidential year until 1832, except in 1820. All parties agreed, however reluctantly, in passing the increased duties, for fear of alienating the votes of the protected interests. In 1820 a tariff was proposed, but failed, because Mr. Monroe was to be re-elected without a contest. As yet, however, in 1816, the question was neither political nor sectional. New England generally opposed the tariff, but not universally. The South acceded to it for the sake of cotton. This article was then heavily taxed abroad, and some very cheap manufactures of it from China and India were largely imported.

It was believed that the development of cotton manufactures here was the best way to make cotton culture lucrative. Lowndes, of South Carolina, reported the bill, and Calhoun made a speech in favor of it. It was based on a report by Dallas, Secretary of the Treasury, in which he divided the articles subject to duty into three classes: (1) those of which the home supply was adequate to the demand; (2) those of which the supply was partial; (3) those of which the supply was small or nothing. He proposed graduated duties on these three classes, the highest duty falling on the first class. You observe at once the incongruity. On the plan of fostering infant industries, duties would evidently be highest on articles producible but not produced, or only slightly produced; but here we find the market closed when the supply is adequate, and only a revenue tax laid on those articles which were least produced, and a medium tax on those which were in the heat of the struggle. It is the best possible test of a theory to see whether it admits of two contradictory applications in practice, for between theory and practice there can be no inconsistency. If any appears, it is proof positive that either the theory or the practice needs revision and correction. To say that a thing is true in theory but bad in practice is a radical absurdity. Theory is the attempt of man to learn general principles for guidance in his practical tasks. Practice is the test of theory, and shows that the general principles have been either correctly or incorrectly apprehended. When, therefore, a theory admits of two opposite applications in practice, one of which fits it as well as the other, it proves conclusively that the theory embraces a contradiction, and we see why protection of infant industries never leads to their independence and to free trade. The advocates of protection use the first form of the theory to secure its adoption and the second to secure its perpetuation.

Calhoun's chief argument for protection was the need of the proposed manufactures in case of war. This argument had considerable force at the end of a war in which foreign supplies had been cut off, but, on the other hand, the exactions of the manufacturers during the war led many to resent any attempt now to favor them.

The argument for protection to provide against the contingency of war has great popular weight. The policy and history of the United States since 1816, however, afford a striking commentary on it. We have always kept our army down a little below the point of efficiency. We have grudged the education of a few officers. We have reduced our navy so low that we hardly do our share in the police of the ocean. We pay little heed to our fortifications. Yet we voluntarily expose ourselves to a loss far greater than the cost of any armament, out of obedience to this notion of providing for a possible war by industrial restraints. Our popular orators formerly made much capital by comparing our expenditures for army, navy and fortifications, with those of the old countries; but they said nothing of this industrial loss incurred to the same end.

Furthermore, is it not a satire on this notion to remember that the only wars in which we have been engaged since 1816 have been that with Mexico and the civil war, in neither of which our cherished industrial independence was of any use to us?

I am not arguing for expenditures on armies and navies. Far from it. We are happy in not needing them. Any one who has to come three thousand miles to fight us will think well of it first. I only point out the grotesque contrast between our preparations for war of the one kind and of the other.

In fact, however, the independence which we seek must be sought in another direction. Independent men are those who have wealth, not those whose houses are stored for a siege. Independent nations are those which are wealthy, because they can command what they want when they want it. Those will be wealthiest which give industry its freest course in time of peace.

The case of the South during the late war is a most striking proof of the fallacy of the "independence" doctrine. The South had less of this artificial independence than any country in the world. It was blockaded and inclosed by an immensely superior force, and what happened? First, people found that when they had put their last stake on war, they could do without thousands of things which had seemed essential; second, they found substitutes and makeshifts to take the place of real essentials; third, they found that, so long as they had commodities to exchange which the rest of the world wanted, no power could prevent the exchange from going on. It does not become those who needed four years to subdue the South to argue that it was weak for lack of industrial independence. Indeed, the argument is incomplete in two or three important points. Suppose that the South had not been weakened by slavery; suppose that it had been an independent nation before and had enjoyed free trade, so that its people had possessed all the wealth they might have accumulated; suppose that its enemy had been obliged to seek it over the ocean, and by sea attack only; on such a hypothesis who can believe that the South would have suffered because it had not "enjoyed protection," and who can urge us, on the chances of ever finding ourselves in the position of the South, to go on creating an artificial independence? Our independence lies in union, good government, and free industry.

The tariff of 1816 was not carried against the instincts of the American people towards freedom without strong opposition. The great majority adhered to the old Jeffersonian doctrines and policy. They wanted to get rid of the army and navy, to reduce taxes and expenditures, to reduce the number of office-holders, and to "let things alone." The prevailing argument was the interest of the existing investments, which, of course, no one desired to destroy. It soon appeared, however, that the barrier of taxation was no equivalent for embargo and war.

The return of peace in Europe allowed industry and finance to return to the operations of natural laws and to escape from the constraints of twenty-five years of war. The shock was terrible, and it took ten years for its effects to subside. In 1816, the English exported immense quantities of manufactured goods to the Continent and to the United States. The results of these transactions were disastrous. Our paper money here also exercised its influence to encourage overtrading and overimportation. In 1817, the manufacturers were in distress. Cries were heard against the inundations of foreign goods, against the drain of specie and against the balance of trade. Evidently we cannot understand these things without taking into account the movements which were going on in the other industrial nations, but the popular opinion here was that the English had set out, by a sacrifice of some millions worth of goods, to destroy American manufactures. This belief had deep root and perhaps has only lately died out, since we have ceased to hear cries of "British gold" whenever any one spoke of free trade. The notion I have referred to received strong re-enforcement from a remark of Brougham's which you may find quoted in the first popular protectionist work you choose to take up, in which he recommended his countrymen to reconquer the American market. If he meant to propose to them to sacrifice their capital in giving several millions' worth of goods to the Americans in order to destroy factories which would spring up again the moment they tried to reimburse themselves, they would have been the first to laugh at him.

An eager effort, however, in favor of protection was now commenced, and it was kept up for fifteen years. It had an organ in Niles' Register, the editor of which was a fanatical protectionist. He filled his paper, week after week, with essays, items, statistics, and arguments in favor of "home industry." No such effort has ever been made on the other side, and I believe that one can understand the means by which the natural tendency of the American people to freedom, and their early bias that way, was perverted, only by observing the zeal and industry with which protectionism was inculcated.

The tariff of 1816 had provided for a gradual decline of the tax on cotton and woolen goods, and Congress had refused to include, as was desired, a prohibition of nankeens, but the time at which the reduction on woolens and cottons was to take place was deferred until 1826, by an Act of April, 20, 1818, and the duty on bar iron was raised from $9 to $15 per ton.

The tariff of 1816 had also adopted the principle of the minimum on cotton cloth, and cotton yarn, none of the former being rated at less than 25 cents per square yard, whatever its cost at the place of exportation. This, of course, cut off the American people from any advantage by the great factory system of England, or from the introduction of machinery in England, so far as these improvements tended to cheapen cotton cloth. It ought to be added that the incorrect valuation of the pound sterling, the inaccuracy of the weights and measures used at this time, and the long credit given by the government for duties, to some extent neutralized the duties.

In 1820, Mr. Baldwin, of Pittsburgh, introduced three bills, one for increased duties, one for taxes on auction sales, and one for cash payment of duties, which all failed to pass. In 1822 and 1823, other bills were introduced for increasing duties, which failed to pass. It was not until the great presidential struggle of 1824 that another tariff crowned the seven years' struggle. Before taking that up I desire to present to you some of the chief doctrines which were believed and taught at this time, as we learn them from the congressional debates and Niles' Register.

It was argued that wages were *not* higher here than in England when properly measured. This was in answer to the free trade argument as then put, that it was useless to try to develop manufactures here because of this disadvantage. Of course, if it is true that wages are higher here, that would be the true inference.

It was also agreed, on behalf of protection, that protection and revenue were antagonistic to each other, and that the government ought to be supported by "direct" taxation, while duties on imports should be reserved entirely for purposes of protection. Niles published long articles in which he urged this view of the subject, and he brought forward many and strong considerations in favor of what he called direct taxation. He showed what the tariff really cost each consumer, he opposed a revenue from import duties as uncertain, and all this in favor of prohibitory duties for the purpose of protection.

Another feature of the controversy was that the shipping interest was blamed in no measured terms for opposing protection to manufactures. The growth of shipping was pointed out and traced back to the discriminating and tonnage duties of 1789, and the shipping interest was charged with selfishness in resisting the application of the same means to other industries. In this connection we meet with the best instance of the fallacy which inheres in the word "protection" itself. In making up the account against the shipping interest for the protection which had been accorded to it, the war undertaken for its defence, but against its will, was charged to it, and also the entire expense of the navy. The navy "protected" the merchant ships from unlawful attacks or interference, that is, it gave them the security which it is the business of government to provide, and which is analogous to the office of courts and police on land, but this protection was made a basis of argument, that the government ought to interfere likewise to "protect" producers *against* *industrial competition.*

A similar charge of selfishness was brought against the cotton manufacturers of New England, who, after 1820, opposed any further protection. Their industry was firmly established and very remunerative, and they found that the effect of protection was simply to disturb their business by tempting great numbers into it, and by exposing it to great fluctuations. It was argued against them that the system ought to be extended to wool and iron, until they reached the same point. This is logical and correct, but, as has often been shown, it reduces the system to an absurdity. After taxing the community to foster one industry, it is proposed to tax that one, with others, to foster a second, then all the preceding to encourage a third. It follows that the first and second lose their advantage, and that the result is a series of weak fosterlings supported by weakened legitimate industries.

The same criticism applies to any system of "incidental protection." The claim is put in to widen the system and do "justice" by favoring all, which is impossible. The only real justice is to favor none.

The great argument of this period, however, was "hard times." There was a commercial crisis in 1819, which has not, perhaps, been equalled since. The complaints were kept up for five years, although the only ground for them, if any, was the comparison with the flush times of speculation and paper money, and they were just such times of distress as the whole commercial world was enduring. The complaints ceased when the tariff of 1824 was passed.

Those who argued most strenuously on this ground, found themselves putting propositions together which made a strange combination when compared. Thus: (1.) The United States is the richest country in the world in point of natural resources, and has only a sparse population. (2.) This favored country is in great distress. (3.) What it needs is more taxation to enable its people to get a living in it.

We not unfrequently find arguments used during this period which show that the speakers or writers believed that a girl in a Manchester factory, who, with a loom, could produce as much cloth as several men could make by hand in the same time, was therefore able to exchange her product for the product of the labor of that number of American farmers. Of course all the notions about the balance of trade, and draining specie, and making money scarce are met with continually.

The duties collected under the tariff of 1816, during the last three years of its operation, were equal to a rate of 30 per cent. on dutiable imports. You see that there had been great progress since Hamilton's day.

I come now to the tariff of 1824. That act would not have been passed if it had not been for the political contest which was impending. Here we meet with the new factor of political intrigue, and also with those phenomena which arise from the extension and complexity of the system. This bill was dexterously combined to embrace strength enough to carry it. We also now find the South opposed to protection; as indeed she had been since 1820. The arguments employed were not new, but the issue was clearer and the debate was far better sustained from the free trade side. We have an argument by Mr. Webster, in which several of the issues which continually arise in this controversy are handled in a masterly manner. He argued them on a plane entirely above the wretched patch-work of which the discussion otherwise consisted. I have already quoted his crushing criticism of the notion of protection as an "American system," under the application of that title which now became current. He showed the advance of opinion on this matter abroad, and showed that we were taking on our young shoulders a load which the older nations would be glad to throw off, if they were not clogged by so many vested interests. He also showed that the distress complained of, so far as it had existed in the last few years, had been due to currency troubles here and abroad, and gave a correct explanation, which few seemed able to understand, of the phenomena of the exchanges here in 1820 and 1821. In regard to the comparative rates of wages, he said: The chairman of the committee "says it would cost the nation nothing, as a nation, to make our ore into iron. Now, I think it would cost us precisely that which we can worst afford; that is, great labor. * * * We have been asked * * in a tone of some pathos, whether we will allow to the serfs of Russia and Sweden the benefit of making our iron for us. Let me inform the gentleman that those same serfs do not earn more than seven cents a day, and that they work in these mines, for that compensation, because they are serfs. And, let me ask the gentleman further, *whether we have any labor in this country that cannot be better employed than in a business which does not yield the laborer more than seven cents a day?* * * * The true reason why it is not our policy to compel our citizens to manufacture our own iron is, that they are far better employed. It is an unproductive business, and they are not poor enough to be obliged to follow it. If we had more of poverty, more of misery and something of servitude; if we had an ignorant, idle, starving population, we might set up for iron makers against the world. * * * The freight of iron has been afforded from Sweden to the United States as low as eight dollars per ton. This is not more than the price of fifty miles' land carriage. Stockholm, therefore, for the purpose of this argument, may be considered as within fifty miles of Philadelphia. Now, it is at once a strong and just view of this case, to consider that there are, within fifty miles of our market, vast multitudes of persons who are willing to labor in the production of this article for us at the rate of seven cents per day, while we have no labor which will not command, upon the average, at least five or six times that amount. The question is then, shall we buy this article of these manufacturers and suffer our own labor to earn its greater reward, or shall we employ our own labor in a similar manufacture, and make up to it, by a tax on consumers, the loss which it must necessarily sustain."

Unfortunately, Mr. Webster was bound by local interests to sustain the protection to shipping, and this was fatal to his opposition. Massachusetts wanted protection on ships, but not on hemp or iron or molasses. A small Massachusetts interest joined with Rhode Island and Connecticut in favor of an increased tax on woolens, but not on wool. The tariff of 1816, it was said, had not sufficiently protected woolens, and had made the tax, such as it was, diminish at intervals. The English bounty on exported woolens was a damage which, it was claimed, ought to be counteracted. Observe the antagonism here established: England, pursuing the old restrictive system by these bounties, made a present to foreign nations at the expense of her own taxpayers. The foreign nations regarded this gift as an injury, and set up barriers against its acceptance, at the expense of their taxpayers. Could anything more conclusively condemn the whole system?

Then look at the internal conflict of interest. Kentucky wanted a tax on hemp to encourage her production, although her dew-rotted hemp was so inferior to the Russian water-rotted hemp that it never competed. She also wanted a tax on molasses to make rum dear in the interest of whiskey. Louisiana wanted a tax on molasses for protection to her sugar planters. The Middle States and Ohio wanted protection on raw wool; and Pennsylvania, of course, wanted protection on iron. In the conflict of interests New England was defeated, having less political power, and hemp, whiskey, iron, and raw wool, uniting the Middle and Western States, carried the day. The minimum on cottons was raised to 30 cts. A minimum for woolens was established at $33\frac{1}{4}$ cts., and the duty was put at 30 per cent., to be advanced to $33\frac{1}{3}$ per cent. in a year. Raw wool, costing less than 10 cts. per lb., was to pay 15 per cent. Other wool was to pay 20 per cent. for a year, 25 per cent. the second year, and 30 per cent. afterwards. Bar iron was raised to $18 per ton if forged, and stood at $30 if rolled. This was to off-set the cheapness of the new process chiefly used in England.

This tariff passed the House by 107 to 102. New England gave 15 votes for it, and 23 against it. The Southern and Southwestern States gave two votes for it. The duties collected under it were, on an average, equal to a rate of 37 per cent.

One expects now, in reading the contemporaneous records, to be rid of the subject for a time. The reader naturally says: "The tariff has been raised; the protection has been granted. The question is disposed of." Nothing of this kind, however, took place. The high-tariff interest was by no means satisfied with the result, especially as regarded woolens. The agitation recommenced the next year, with a reiteration of the old arguments, condemnation of "our present ruinous system," and demand for protection, as if there had been no concessions in that direction. This calls our attention to certain features inherent in the protective system, and shows us how erroneous in practice, as well as in theory, is the notion that we can proceed through protection to free trade. Protection nourishes dependence, not independence. It is a system in which all the parts hang together, and protection for some cannot be united with freedom for others. If one industry should be set out in free competition, while the rest were protected, it would be found that they are interdependent; that machinery, raw materials and labor supplies would be so dear that the exposed industry would have no fair chance in competition with foreigners. Hence one long protected industry, if it became independent by natural causes, could not be left free unless the whole system were abandoned. But then the cry goes up from those nurslings of recent beginning, that they are not yet ready. If you defer the introduction of freedom for ten years longer on their account, a new company of infants is meantime brought into being, and the plea for further delay comes from them. Thus you go on forever, and the theory is reduced to an absurdity.

During the period from 1824 to 1828 the political factor in the tariff controversy rose to chief importance. The administration of J. Q. Adams was exposed to the most vigorous and relentless opposition from the party which had formed around Andrew Jackson. After the Democratic convention of Harrisburg in 1824 it was certain that Pennsylvania was enthusiastic for Jackson. The rural population of that State cared more for Jackson than for tariff. This was a fact which the politicians had simply to accept as a fact. The composition of the Jackson party, therefore, coincided to a certain extent with the coalition which had passed the tariff of 1824. New England as the Adams section was, both politically and on the tariff, still more in a position to be neglected than it was in 1847. The South found its political combinations and its tariff interests inconsistent.

England still furnished a convenient and popular object of attack. She now showed her perfidy and desire to ruin American manufactures by reducing her own duties on raw wool to one penny per lb. This enabled her manufacturers to manufacture so cheaply as to pay our import duties and yet compete with success. According to the theory which we are studying, this was a serious reason for "protecting" ourselves against the good this might have brought to us. The woolen manufacturers of Boston accordingly sent a petition to Congress in 1826 asking for more protection. Jan. 10th, 1827, a bill was introduced for raising the duties on wool and woolens. It was tabled in the Senate by the casting vote of Calhoun. It was in the New England interest, and, as Niles said, politics were in the way.

In July, 1827, a national convention met at Harrisburg, called by the Pennsylvania Society for the Promotion of Manufactures and Mechanic Acts to consider measures for promoting manufactures. It was the most energetic attempt ever made to organize and give symmetry to the protectionist movement. It adopted resolutions in favor of more protection for iron, steel, glass, wool, woolens and hemp. It proposed a duty of 20 cents a pound on wool costing 8 cents or more, to advance 2½ cents per annum until it should be 50 cents. It adopted four minima for woolens, 50 cents, $2.50, $4.00, $6.00. The duty was to be 40 per cent. for a year, 45 per cent. the next year, and 50 per cent. afterwards.

The committee on manufactures at the next session of Congress recommended that evidence should be taken as to the state of manufactures. This was a new departure, for hitherto all tariff legislation had been made blindly and ignorantly. The Northern protectionists opposed the proposition; the South favored and carried it. The evidence all went to show deplorable distress in all manufacturing industry, although the country generally was enjoying great prosperity. The argument necessarily was tangled and contradictory. It was urged, and really was the greatest popular argument, that the country owed its prosperity to the tariff, but here were the manufacturers claiming to be in distress. The truth was that the country possessed such means of producing wealth that the tariff could not crush them. Then again the distress was needed as an argument for more protection, but what light did it throw back on the previous attempts in that direction?

Many of the peculiar doctrines I have mentioned as advocated at an earlier period were now heard no longer, but a new one was brought forward and repeated again and again, viz., that protection, by domestic competition, lowers prices. I have already, in my former lecture, discussed this doctrine.

The new tariff bill was introduced in February, 1828. It was based upon the recommendations of the Harrisburg convention. Its central feature was wool and woolens. Hemp, iron and molasses figured as before. It came forward, therefore, as a New England or Adams measure, and the Jackson coalition opposed it, but under the necessity of satisfying the Middle and Western States. The feeling in the South was already very bitter about the tariff legislation, and this new effort to push on the system, reckless of Southern protests, still further embittered the South. The West also took the position that they had as yet had nothing of this good, which it was assumed that the Government had to distribute, and they demanded that, if the system was to go on, they should have their share. Mr. Webster took the position for Massachusetts, that she had been forced into manufactures by the policy adopted in 1824, in spite of her protests, and she now protested that the investments into which she had been drawn should not be sacrificed.

You look in vain through the discussion of this bill for any broad principles. Much was said indeed about a national policy, but it all referred to this system which, at the first approach to actual discussion, resolved itself into political intrigue, a strife of sections, and a struggle between "interests." Much was said about broad principles, but all referred to the notion that by robbing all for the benefit of the few it was possible in some way, which never was explained, to gain great benefit to all. The South adopted the policy of trying to make the bill as bad as possible. They proposed and advocated absurd and extravagant exaggerations, in the hope, apparently, that they could thus make apparent to the protectionists the enormity of their propositions and the absurdity of their demands. This policy did not work. The belief in the great protectionist dogmas had now become strong. Political exigencies were great, and the Northern protectionists either rejected the exaggerated propositions, or accepted them in good faith. This tariff came to be known as the "tariff of abominations," but its worst abominations were forced into it by the perverse policy of the Southern men. What it concerns us to observe is, the evil effects of mixing up politics and president-making with fiscal legislation, and the exaggerations to which the protective system leads.

The result of this struggle was that the tax on molasses was raised to 10 cents per gallon. The tax on wool was put at 4 cents per pound and 40 per cent., to increase by 5 per cent. annually until it was 50 per cent. A $1.00 minimum was inserted in the scheme proposed at Harrisburgh, and a tax of 40 cents a square yard was laid. This combination of taxes, resulting from political motives only, to favor the wool growers of the Middle and Ohio States and not to make woolens dear to consumers in the same districts and in the South, was exceedingly injurious to woolen manufacturers. You observe that it is not in human ingenuity to interpose in the delicate relations of trade by arbitrary enactments without doing damage. On account of these features of the tariff in regard to molasses and woolens it got only 16 votes from New England (in the House) to 23 against it.

The tax on bar iron, not rolled, was raised to $22.40 per ton; if rolled,

$37 per ton. Hemp was raised to $45 per ton. These features, with the tax on wool, gained the force which carried the bill in the house, 105 to 94. On the final vote, there were in the affirmative 61 Adams and 44 Jackson votes; in the negative, 35 Adams and 59 Jackson votes. The South, after putting the "abominations" in the bill, voted against it, except three votes. To show the want of good faith, it is significant to notice that, on the motion for the previous question, 11 Adams and 99 Jackson men voted in the affirmative, and 80 Adams and 11 Jackson men in the negative.

All the New England men, and all the *bona fide* tariff men like Niles were disatisfied with this bill, and began at once to agitate for its amendment. It has been customary for the tariff advocates to speak of it as a good bill, which only needed some slight "adjustments." We see, I think, if we look at it candidly, the very best proof that such adjustments are required forever, that is, that they are impossible. It is a specimen of the purest quackery in legislation. I think it shows also that the only petition any sober business man can ever address to the Legislature is to "let him alone" and, if possible, not legislate about his affairs at all. In this very debate of 1828, Mr. Stevenson, of Pennsylvania, arguing for the tariff, said : "If legislation were as intelligent as commerce is vigilant, much national evil might be avoided." I could only improve this by saying : "If it were perceived that legislation never can be as intelligent as commerce is vigilant, far more national evil would be avoided."

The agitation of the Northern protectionists, for the amendment of the tariff, sank into insignificance in comparison with the discontent which the tariff caused in the South. The South was, of course, crippled by slavery, but it is undeniable that the complaint the Southerners made was just and well founded. They sold in a free market and bought in a protected one. They claimed that they had inherited the grievances of the colonies at the revolution, and that they stood just where the colonists had stood at that time; asking why they should maintain a political connection in which the taxing power was abused for their oppression. When they were told that they must yield to the welfare of the whole, they replied that this was England's old argument that the colonies should bow to imperial considerations. Thus the tariff controversy, pushed to extremes by the power of the majority, and in disregard of the pleas of the minority for justice, assailed our political system in its most delicate and most vital part—the integrity of the confederation. The attempt of South Carolina to nullify the tariff act was not open disunion and secession. It was worse. It was an attempt to remain in the Union and yet reduce the confederation to imbecility and contempt. Thus forty years after the first tariff with its 8 per cent. import on dutiable, we find that the system had steadily advanced, that the infant industries were as feeble and clamorous as ever, that the burden had been increased until it was now equal to 41 per cent., that it had been elaborated into a system in which the lobby had been trained and educated, that it had corrupted politics and furnished capital for political schemes, that it had, on the testimony of those interested, done them no good, and that it had brought the confederation face to face with its greatest danger, that of disruption.

LECTURE V.

VACILLATION OF THE PROTECTION POLICY IN THIS COUNTRY.—
CONCLUSION.

At the point which I have now reached, in my review of the history of protection in the United States, it is necessary to observe that the original prejudice of the Americans in favor of liberty of every kind had been crushed out as regards trade. The frequent changes of the tariff had educated the generation which had grown up since the second war to the dogmas and fallacies of protection. These had been preached assiduously by Niles and Carey, and being plausible and popular, and falling in with national prejudices, they had gained great currency. There had, indeed, been no argument for the other side. We are familiar with the fact that a special interest finds ardent advocates and energetic workers, while the public interest lacks defenders.

In 1829, Condy Raguet commenced the publication of the *Free Trade Advocate*, in which he published some of the best writing on financial and economic topics ever produced on this side the water. He wrote above his readers, for whose minds Niles' style and arguments were much better adapted, and his journal soon expired. He continued his work in another journal, called the *Banner of the Constitution*, for some time longer.

Another fact, which it is important to observe for a correct understanding of the movement in this country towards protectionism, is the great prosperity which was enjoyed here from the second war until 1837. The advantages of the new country were, of course, enormous, and every improvement in transportation and every new invention tended to bring them within reach. The losses inflicted by a bad tariff belonged in the great margin of what might have been. The people had not lost something which they once had. They had fallen short of something which they might have possessed for the labor they had expended. This is something which people are slow to understand. Rob them of a good which they have possessed, or diminish comforts to which they have been accustomed, and they feel it. They are slower to understand that a given amount of labor might have produced, under a given condition of society, a certain result, and that they have fallen short of it. Such, however, is the correct statement of the effect of any tariff system, and the American people have always been slow to understand it, because they have enjoyed so much, and have been growing in comfort so steadily, that they could almost afford to be indifferent to something still better.

In 1830, this prosperity was pointed to in vindication of the tariff system, and with great popular effect. The fact was that the circumstances were so favorable that legislation could only lessen, not cripple, the advantages, but it was said that the tariff had caused all the prosperity, and hence the argument was: Let us have more. In the session of 1830–31 some efforts were made to strengthen the tariff of 1828. For instance, it was proposed to repeal the provision that the tax on salt should be reduced from 10 to 5 cents, January 1, 1832, and to raise it to 15 cents.

In the fall of 1831, two national conventions, one of protectionists and one of free traders, were held. The free traders met at Philadelphia, September 30, and published a clear and sound address, setting forth the simple principles, which are all mere truisms, and must rely on common sense for their effect. The effect seems to have been very slight. The Tariff convention met at New York, Oct. 26. It published an address, and appointed committees to collect and publish "reports" on various industries. The address consisted of bad political economy and the usual special pleas to bar the common sense application of simple principles. As a specimen, I quote a single sentence : " Nations are adversary to each other. Their commercial intercourse is regulated by treaties always made with a view to relative advantages, and to provide for those hostilities which are of perpetual occurrence." The "reports" offered jumbled and immaterial statistics about amounts produced and amounts imported, and had their corner-stone in one on "the balance of trade" view of the currency. They all talk of the calamity of buying without selling, an operation which we are accustomed to call, in the rare cases when we experience it, receiving presents, and they go into hysterics about the damage endured from foreigners who send their surplus stocks here and sacrifice them at auction, which is only declaiming against cheapness.

In the session of 1831–2, a presidential election approaching, the whole subject came up again. The Committee on Ways and Means presented a majority and minority report, with bills. The Committee on Manufactures proposed a high tariff revision. The Secretary of the Treasury reported a more moderate bill. The Senate also had a bill. There were also numerous amendments. The result was a remodeled tariff adjusted to suit the protective policy, signed July 14, 1832.

This, then, was the answer to Southern protests. The Southern position was doubly unfortunate. In the first place, they insisted on the unconstitutionality of the tariff, and sought nullification as a remedy. This complicated their position with the most difficult and vital constitutional questions. In the second place, they did not fight intelligently for free trade, nor yet for a revenue tariff. They wanted a "horizontal tariff," and *ad valorem* duties. South Carolina called a convention in November, 1832, and persisted in movements towards nullifying the tariff. The President met them with a proclamation setting forth his duty and intentions. Congress met again in that year with the question of tariff in the first place of interest. A bill introduced by Mr. Verplanck was intended to conciliate. Many and serious amendments altering its character were introduced, and the whole winter was spent in struggles over them. Suddenly, near the end of the session, Mr. Clay proposed another bill to supersede them all. Mr. Calhoun had quarreled with the President, and had been thrown into opposition, and he and Mr. Clay arranged the compromise under circumstances which are differently stated by different authorities. The day before that on which the Act of July was to go into operation, March 2, 1833, this compromise tariff was signed by the President. It provided that the taxes fixed by the tariff of 1832, so far as the *ad valorem* rates exceeded twenty per cent., should be reduced by one-tenth of the excess over twenty per cent. on the first of January in each alternate year until 1841. In that year they were to be reduced one-half of the remaining excess, and in 1842, were to be reduced to twenty per cent. This would issue, of course, in a horizontal tariff at that rate. This bill also shortened the period of credits on imports, and raised the custom house valuation of the sovereign to $4.80. The reduction operated only slowly. It started from the stringent high tariff of 1832, and the " horizontal" tariff had no principle of protection, or free trade, or revenue in it. The compromise was a pure political makeshift, in which the public and private interests had no consideration.

Now, one looks with great interest through the history of the subsequent years to see if manufactures died out. One expects lugubrious descriptions of disasters from the protectionist journals. Nothing of this kind, however, is to be found. Niles drops his long essays. The subject disappears from his columns. No disasters take place. The woes of the woollen men are forgotten. The simple fact is that when Congress had put the question aside, the manufacturers ceased to carry on their business in the lobby, but attended to it at home. They probably found this more profitable. At any rate they prospered, and the whole country prospered steadily until the currency errors came in once more to produce disaster.

The panic of 1837, and the bank crash of 1839, spread ruin throughout the country. This is not the place to speak of the causes or relations of this disaster. Suffice it to say, that great amounts of capital had been invested here by Europeans during the last decade, and that a vast indebtedness had been incurred on a bank inflation. The capital had been largely invested in internal improvements carried on by a kind of mania. These works were often unwisely undertaken and extravagantly conducted. They offered no promise of profit. Correctly regarded, however, this disaster was the result of rash and ignorant abuse of exuberant natural advantages, but the abuse had been so excessive that the revulsion was terrible, and the country did not recover for five years.

I take no account here of the various attempts which were made during the period of the compromise to alter the duties, either directly or under the form of bills to secure the collection of the revenue. It is sufficient to say that there were several such attempts, and that the compromise did not run its course without signs of the old longing to legislate on this subject. The last years of the period, when the duties were lowest, fell in with the distress of 1837 to 1842. The old argument of "hard times," therefore came up with renewed force in favor of more protection. People did not see that when a country like this, enjoying the greatest natural advantages, suffers distress, it is proof positive that artificial and legislative arrangements must have interfered injuriously with the play of natural laws. I cannot too strenuously insist upon this, in view of present circumstances. The soil of the earth furnishes the necessaries and comforts of life when man applies labor and capital to get them out of it. If one man has much land at his disposal, he can get abundance with little labor. He pays all the persons engaged in manufactures, trade, transportation and personal services out of his abundance, for saving him from loss, or doing part of his work for him, or contributing to his comfort and advantage. This is a simple statement of the economic organization of modern society. It regulates itself perfectly. The natural laws, the law of value, the law of exchange, the principle of free contract, are sufficient to keep the whole system in harmonious operation. If the resources of the soil are inadequate to the demands, either because population is excessive or the soil poor, the way of escape is by emigration or an improvement in the arts; but if the soil is rich, and the population meager, and yet there is distress, the place to look for the causes is in the artificial arrangements of man. We must have misapprehended the laws of nature which govern economic circumstances, and put our legislative enactments out of joint with them. The way out of trouble lies in a closer study of the science of economy, and a more correct adjustment of our arrangements to the laws which it teaches. The general custom of man is, however, to try to correct one bad arrangement by another, to put another cog, or another lever, or another spring, into the machine, never remembering that he thus simply increases the friction, and lessens the force which he had before. It has long been generally known that we cannot invent a perpetual motion, because it is making something out of nothing, but in social and economic arrangements, analogous efforts are still continually made. So it was in 1842. Distress prevailing, it was supposed to be the business of government to remove distress. What else, it was asked, did government exist for? It was a paternal, fostering institution. To be sure, the persons who composed it as individuals, enjoyed, with a few exceptions, but little respect. The functions which legitimately belonged to government were notoriously ill-performed. It did worse, and at far greater expense, whatever it tried to do, than any person or corporation in the country. If it possessed any occult force, or any superior intelligence, or any improved machinery for getting what men want in this world, it certainly kept it secret and produced no proofs of it. Yet the superstition of government, then and still strong amongst us, led people to look to government to do for them what they could only do for themselves by industry and economy.

The whigs entertained the general conception that government demeaned itself when it narrowed its own functions. They believed in the paternal theory. They scorned all the notions which had prevailed in the government for twelve years, and, having won a victory in 1840, they were eager to put their own theory in practice. They passed a bill for distributing the proceeds of the public lands amongst the States, thus stripping the government of a legitimate source of revenue; but it was provided that this distribution should not take place when duties were above twenty per cent. At the next session (1842) they passed a provisional tariff with a clause repealing the limitation on distribution, but it was vetoed by Mr. Tyler. They then passed a permanent tariff, which he also vetoed; both on account of the repeal of the limitation on distribution. They then passed the tariff of August 30th, 1842, raising duties and cutting off distribution. This act turned back to protection. It was based on the tariff of 1832, but the duties were lower. The reviving industries of the country, consequent on the destruction of the bad currency, and the restoration of sound values, were pointed at as proofs of the success of this policy.

The arguments employed at this period offer nothing new. The notion, so prevalent in 1832, that high tariffs lower prices, and which was then affirmed as a broad and general truth, was little heard in 1842. The grounds put forward at the latter date were the old and worn out fallacies about imports and exports, balance of trade, drain of specie, &c., &c. A specimen from the report of the Committee on Manufactures may suffice: "There are several causes for the present depression of property and general stagnation of business, one of which will be admitted to be the large amount of our importations over the amount of exports. This depresses our home industry and draws from the country annually large balances in specie, crippling our banks and depriving them of the power to grant necessary facilities." A great part of the public documents of the United States consist in a reiteration and expansion of this paragraph, every clause of which contains errors which are refuted in any standard elementary text book on political economy. The importations cannot exceed the exportations over any period of time. If they do for a time, it is proof that they ought to, and it cannot produce any stagnation in business. If imported articles drive home manufactures out of the market, it only proves that the people are getting their supplies cheaper, and that that particular form of home industry is falling behind in the industrial race. We have only the alternative of letting the persons interested do as we all have to do, employ energy and skill to sustain themselves, or else rob ourselves to protect them in inferiority—that is to subsidize negligence, inefficiency and want of skill. The importations cannot "draw away specie" unless we part with it willingly; and if we do, we give up what is worth less for what is worth more. We cannot be robbed of specie except by an invading army, and if we give it up in trade, we give it up for a profit. No sound bank, which has not by its excessive issues injured commerce and industry, can be "crippled" by an export of specie, and such an export is the proper protection of the public against the injury which excessive bank issues are doing. As for lessening the power of the banks to "grant necessary facilities," the committee are under that notion of banks which regards them as beneficent institutions whose function is to create capital for people who want it.

By the election of Polk in 1844 the South gained control of the government. In 1845 the cry was raised that the tariff was in danger. Meetings were held to protest against any change. The project of Mr. Walker, Secretary of the Treasury, was the old southern plan of horizontal rates and *ad valorem* duties. He divided nearly all imports into eight schedules with duties at 100, 40, 30, 25, 20, 15, 10 and 5 per cent. *ad valorem*. This bill passed the House 114 to 94, and the Senate 28 to 27, after a debate and a public excitement, different in kind but scarcely less in degree than that of 1832. The average rate of duty under it was 25½ per cent. on dutiable, until 1857. By the Act of March 3, 1857, the duties were lowered to an average rate of 20¼ per cent on dutiable.

The period from 1846 to 1860 was our period of comparative free trade. The Sub-Treasury Act of 1846 removed subjects of currency and banking from national legislation. Thus these two topics were for a time laid aside. For an industrial history of the United States, no period presents greater interest than this. It was a period of very great and very solid prosperity. The tariff was bad and vexatious in many ways, if we regard it from the standpoint either of free trade or revenue tariff, but its rates were low and its effects limited. It was called " a revenue tariff with incidental protection." The manufactures which, it had been said, would perish, did not perish, and did not gain sudden and exorbitant profits. They made steady and genuine progress. The repeal of the English corn laws in 1846 opened a large market for American agricultural products, and took away the old argument which Niles and Carey had used with such force, that England wanted other countries to have free trade, but could not take their products. The effect on both countries was most happy. It seemed as if the old system was gone forever, and that these two great nations, with free industry and free trade, were to pour increased wealth upon each other. The fierce dogmatism of protection and its deeply-rooted prejudices seemed to have undergone a fatal blow. Our shipping rapidly increased. Our cotton crop grew larger and larger. The discovery of gold in California added mightily to the expansion of prosperity. The states indeed repeated our old currency follies, and the panic of 1857 resulted, but it was only a stumble in a career of headlong prosperity. We recovered from it in a twelvemonth. Slavery agitation marked this period politically, and if people look back to it now they think most of that; but industrially and economically, and I will add also, in the administration of the government, the period from the Mexican to the civil war is our golden age, if we have any. There was simplicity, even to dullness, in national affairs. It was one of those happy periods when a nation has little history. As far as the balance of trade is concerned, it never was more regular and equal than in this period.

The Act of March 3, 1857, was called for, because the revenue had risen beyond the necessities of the government, and the debt had been reduced to an insignificant sum. The bill lowered duties about one quarter, and applied especially to raw materials of manufacture. In the debate, however, strong opposition to it was aroused, and no little old protectionism was called out. The West objected to the reduction on raw materials, especially wool, hemp and lead, which they produced, and threatened to resist the incidental protection to Eastern manufactures. This brought out the weakness and error of incidental protection in strong light. So long as there is *any* protection the argument is sure to arise under this form. Those who are not protected demand that revenue be raised from products similar to theirs in order to give them a share in the incidental benefit. In short we are forced either to protect all or to protect none, and we see distinctly that there is no safe position to take except that of total opposition to all protection. If we lay any duties which act protectively, we must offset them by excise taxes, that no benefit may accrue.

Congress was divided in 1857 between two policies for the reduction of revenue, and was embarrassed by a novel difficulty in legislation, that of getting rid of a surplus which threatened worse demoralization than any public debt. It was then fully perceived that by reducing taxes revenue was increased. The tariff of '46 had been estimated to yield about twenty millions. The receipts from it in 1856 were over sixty millions. It was therefore urged that, to reduce revenue, duties ought to be raised and used for protection.

The panic of 1857, of course, reduced imports and lessened revenue.

In 1858 there was a recovery, which was still greater in 1859. In 1860 political troubles produced another reduction. The expenses of the government in the meantime increased and a deficit arose. This formed the basis for the new effort to increase duties. The real motive, however, was political. The Republican party wanted to make sure of Pennsylvania. That state was aware of its value to the Union and to the party in question. As a member of the Confederation, no one would have esteemed it less than any other, but it was still in the position of a member of the family who wants to live on the contributions of the others. It added to the incongruity of the situation that this member claimed to be possessed of means of wealth surpassing all the others, but he could not get a living out of them. He would not be idle either, but insisted on sinking capital in unproductive enterprises and calling on his brethren to make up his losses.

The Republican party made the bargain. Mr. Morrill introduced his tariff in the House, March 12th, 1860, and it was passed. The Senate postponed it to the next session. In June, the Chicago Convention adopted a tariff plank. The bill came up at the next session and passed the Senate February 20th, 1861, by a vote of 25 to 14, seven Southern States having, up to that time, seceded. The bill passed the House promptly by a large vote, and was signed March 2d, 1861. It went into operation April 1st. It raised duties from the tariff of 1857 about one-third. The debate hinged upon revenue almost entirely and showed the result of fourteen years' education in comparative free trade.

This fact is well worth observing. Ten to fifteen years suffice to change the voting population and to educate a generation in one set of ideas or another. Thus the traditions of one policy secure a certain stability within that period and men lose memory of any other. It is always difficult for men to realize in imagination, or by description, a social condition other than that they have experienced. The power to do this is only acquired by study and travel. Hence it is to-day that most people acquiesce in the paper money and protectionist fallacies to which we have, as a generation, become accustomed.

The Morrill tariff does not call for any extended notice, because it only lasted four months. A new act became a law on August 5th, 1861, which raised duties from the date of its passage. It was a revenue act, but contained many protectionist jobs. The immediate result was that it produced effects on trade which legislators, inexperienced in this department and ignorant of the laws of taxation, did not foresee, and it stimulated numberless efforts to secure for other "interests" similar advantages. Another act of December 24th, 1861, increased the taxes on tea, coffee and sugar.

In 1862 the internal taxes were laid. They were extended from time to time without method or intelligence, but they proved conclusively enough that that system of taxation is perfectly feasible in this country, and that, on a system adjusted to the best modern principles of taxation. it could be used here as well or better than anywhere else in the world. It was unpopular and produced grumbling, which is one of its chief recommendations, because people knew what they were paying, and they were guarded against the apathy which characterizes them in regard to import duties. The latter are far more mischievous, but are paid unconsciously. The time will come, in the advance of enlightenment, when men will demand to be allowed to conduct their business in entire freedom. so as to make as much as they can, and then pay taxes which they must pay out of the net proceeds, and when they would as soon let the grocer and butcher draw on their bank accounts without presenting a bill, as let the government put its hands in their pockets for taxes when they do not know it. It would be an amusing experiment if this government should for a year exact by internal taxes without duties the same sum which the tariff now costs us, and then pay in bounties to the protected interests the sum which they now get.

The Act of July 14, 1862, raised duties "temporarily." The joint resolution of April 29th, 1864, raised all duties fifty per cent. for sixty days, afterwards extended to ninety. The Act of June 30th, 1864, was a general revision for revenue and protection. It was represented as 'a necessary offset to the internal duties and as a temporary war tariff.' The Act of March 3d, 1865, again extended and complicated the system by more minute subdivisions and classifications and by enhanced rates. It involved a number of tricks and devices intended to have an effect which could not be foreseen, and was a reckless exertion of the powers which had been rediscovered as latent in this kind of legislation. The Act of July 28th, 1866, revised and strenghtened the last act, by various provisions intended to clinch its operation.

These are the acts which belong directly to the war period. The people were busy in war making; their attention was absorbed in that direction. Congress itself was so absorbed in this business that the questions involved in tariff did not obtain consideration. The necessity of getting revenue was paramount, and there was no scientific knowledge of the principles of taxation to govern the attempt. The only system employed was to tax everything, and if more revenue was wanted, to tax more heavily. The people submitted patriotically, because they thought it necessary. The abundance of paper money, with rising prices and great speculation, created enormous fortunes and produced a semblance of prosperity. People thought that millions of men could leave industry and go to destroying capital, and yet the nation get rich. Under such circumstances the natural consequence was that the social parasites found a grand opportunity. We must distinguish here two kinds of protection; the doctrinaire protection of Clay, Niles, Carey and Greeley, which was *bona fide* belief in the doctrine as a theory of national wealth, and the interested protection of cliques and individuals, who employ the system only for selfish ends. The latter was the kind which arose here ten years ago and under which we are now living. We enjoyed the services, as national legislators, of Mr. Morrell and Mr. Stevens, Pennsylvania iron masters; Mr. McCarthy, for the New York Salt Works; Mr. Morrill, for the Vermont sheep raisers. Our Congress was beset by lobbyists, who found it easier to speculate by moving legislation than by cornering the market; and to look at our legislation it seemed that we were a confederation only for the sake of holding a grand scramble at Washington to see which section and which interest should worst plunder the rest.

The system was elaborated as a "temporary" system—as a war measure—like the paper money, and we have been living under it ever since. Too many people find their interest in sustaining it to let it fall without a struggle, on behalf of the great public which elects all the Congressmen, but finds few representatives. The internal taxes, which formed the excuse for a large part of the advance in duties have been gradually abolished, and the whole weight of destructive restraint is left to fall on the industries of the country. Evidently the whole policy was erroneous and false, even from the point of view adopted. In going into a great war, the nation wanted its powers free. It wanted cheapness and abundance then, if ever. It wanted the maximum of revenue according to the most approved methods of obtaining it. It was no time to re-undertake the task of encouraging industries, even if that ever was wise, and I believe that the historian, when he comes to criticise this period in our history, will say that the welfare of a great nation never was so recklessly sacrificed by ignorant empiricism in legislation, nor the patriotism of a great people ever so wantonly abused, as in the tariff legislation of our war. Our position then and since as to tariff and paper money always reminds me of one of the blessings of Jacob: "Issachar is a strong ass, bowed down between two burdens. And he saw that rest was good, and the land that it was pleasant, and bowed his shoulders to bear, and became a servant unto tribute."

I come now, however, to the most shameful chapter in the whole story. In 1867, the woolen manufacturers being dissatisfied with the protection they enjoyed, held a convention at Syracuse to exert the influence which was due to the importance of their industry on legislation. Upon their arrival, they met with an unexpected obstacle. Lo! there were also the representatives of the wool-growers. These latter had come to watch and to say that they must be counted in. Obviously, the path of wisdom lay in an alliance. An adjustment to satisfy the wool-growers was made, and the tax on woolens was put enough higher to allow for this. The tariff there concocted was enacted into a law March 2d, 1867. It consisted of a minute classification, and a complicated graduated rate which has tormented the woolen industry ever since. In 1868 and 1869, we saw mutton a drug on the market at 8 and 9 cts., when beef was 20. The farmers who had been deluded into relying on tariffs to produce wealth, found that they had to send their sheep to slaughter.

The woolen interest profited no better. They had to import dirt from Australia when they wanted wool. If the price advanced, or any turn of exchange or item of cost carried the total cost over 12 cts., they found a higher rate of duty exacted, and the importation unprofitable. When they turned to the home supply they found that it was all on one grade, and that they were deprived of the advantage of mixing wools to make various fabrics. Mills were started by ignorant and inexperienced persons in improper places, and the supply of cloth, all on one grade, glutted the market. In 1869 a crisis in the industry occurred, with numerous failures. Mills were sold out for a fraction of their cost. New proprietors started, with a smaller capital account, and there has since been nothing but a struggling and unremunerative existence for this industry.

In 1870 the first reduction of duties took place, and it was on the debate of this bill that the old divergence as to the principle of protection reappeared. The sections and interests were so completely included in the system that there was little clear, complete and outspoken advocacy of free trade, such as the South used to offer. Almost every member had a reservation in favor of the interest of his own district. It only proves again that the system must be assailed as a whole. Pig iron was reduced from $9 to $7 per ton. The other reductions were chiefly on tea, coffee, sugar, spices, wines and fruits, things which ought to bear taxes if anything does. In 1872, 10 per cent. was taken from the duty on some of the most important articles in the tariff, but the amount was restored in the session of 1874-5, by what was called the "little tariff" bill. The tariff now contains 1,500 articles and specifications. In 1874 the average rate was equivalent to 38½ per cent. on dutiable imports.

In the mean time American shipping had ceased to be. Other nations bought shipping and sailed it at a profit, if they could not build it. We prohibited this. Nevertheless, under even this utmost exertion of the restrictive system, the revival of our shipping, longingly looked for and often promised, never came. Our flag is kept afloat by one or two subsidized lines, and by one on a course which other shipowners have abandoned as unprofitable. Perhaps the Pacific Mail Line enlists the pride of Americans. From time to time it is proposed to go on and subsidize ships, in order to force the long-desired revival. This is consistent at least. Having taxed tonnage in foreign trade out of existence, and forbidden the transfer of foreign built ships to American registers in order to spite the shipowners who abandoned our flag during the war, we now propose to tax agriculture and commerce back again to provide a fund for subsidizing ships.

Our exports have likewise been killed by the inevitable operation of the tariff. We no longer offer a market and cannot attract miscellaneous orders. We cannot export to countries whose products we do not take. We cannot trade directly with South America, the East Indies, or Australia, even for the exports in which we could doubtless compete in those markets, because we refuse to take their products. We cannot make round voyages because no one could tell what would be done with the tariff at home during the interval which must elapse. Our manufacturers having secured the home market, find that the home market becomes a restraint, not an advantage, and they move out of the country in order to get rid of the trammels of the tariff while working for export. Our own sewing machines are provided for foreign nations cheaper than we can get them ourselves. The system has been pushed so far, and its complicated developments have become so interlocked with each other that the protective system is to-day a dead weight on all the production of the country of every kind. Its complete overthrow would be a grand emancipation for manufactures as well as for everything else.

How far we yet are from anything like this movement was shown a few weeks ago by the proposition gravely made, and, it appears, gravely entertained at Washington, to lay discriminating duties so as to bear on the civil war in the Island of Cuba. The taxing power is the greatest engine controlled by governments, and it has been used or abused to aid temperance, to restrain luxury, to put down slavery (the English discriminating duties on slave-grown sugar), to coerce belligerents in favor of neutrals, and, in this last case, is proposed to accomplish an interference in a foreign struggle with which we could not interfere justifiably in any way.

This completes the hasty review which I have been able, under the circumstances, to give of the history of our tariff legislation. Some things seem to follow from it so evidently that no one can contradict them.

In the first place this notion that there is some means to increase, by an adjustment of taxes, the wealth of a country has had a very full trial amongst us. It was inherited by us from older countries, in which the pressure of population on the means of subsistence was great, and the idea of the functions of government wide. It was hostile to all the beliefs and habits of thought of the American people. It was totally incongruous with the social and political system which they established. It was reluctantly admitted under the idea that a new country may need some stimulus and assistance at the outset. In this view it is forgotten that the stimulus must come from without to be of any use, and that, if it is sought within, it can only be obtained by depressing one part to develop another. Nothing is created by the system, nor ever can be. It is only another instance of the folly which we continually commit of trying to make something out of nothing, or to lift ourselves by our bootstraps. As I have shown, the curtailment and depression fell in the United States on agriculture. In England it fell on manufactures for the benefit of agriculture, and in any country, old or new, the doctrine holds absolutely, that whatever means of wealth it has, and whatever the kind may be, they work up to their maximum when they work freely.

The Americans adopted the notion, however, that they could, by a few years of self-denial, get certain industries started, which would then "go alone" and become independent sources of wealth. I not only affirm on the grounds of reason and science that such a theory is absurd and fallacious, but I now appeal to the century of history as a complete proof that there is something wrong and false about this theory. Where are the results? Instead of strong, independent industries, we have to-day only a hungry and clamorous crowd of "infants." We are told that our country is rich in everything good for man, and every new discovery of natural sources of wealth is made the ground, not of greater abundance and less labor, but of greater scarcity and greater labor. Find a mine of copper in the United States, and it is an argument for making it harder for the people of the United States to get copper than before. We used to get emery to supply all our wants by giving wheat and cotton for it; we did not know we had any. At length a bed of ore was found in Massachusetts, and the first step was to get legislation to make the American people give more wheat and tobacco for emery than before. The same applies to all our great resources, until it might be worth while to calculate how much more iron, coal, copper and lead the people of the United States would have to-day, if there was not a particle of either under their soil, than they now possess. There is immense force, apparently, in the fallacy that we want "industries," when in fact we want goods to supply our needs; in the idea that we want work, when in fact we want leisure. We are trying to sustain life on the face of the earth, and we find it hard work. All our discoveries and inventions have for their object to make it easier; that is, to get more goods for the same labor, and to sustain more, or more highly developed, men. For this we want leisure from drudgery, as the first and most imperative requisite. Therefore, everything which gets the goods and lessens the labor is an advance in civilization; and everything which makes more labor necessary to get the goods tends to barbarism. Labor for material good is simply a gross necessity, which we are all the time trying to conquer in order to get leisure for pleasanter and higher occupation, and, above all else, it follows that those whose lives are all spent in drudgery over material needs are most clogged in their efforts for emancipation by everything which increases labor. Hence this aim with which the early American statesmen set out has proved a chimera. The further we follow it, the further it leads us. We get more industry and less good.

It follows, secondly, from this history that this continual law-making about industry has been prolific of industrial and political mischief. It has tainted our political life with log-rolling, presidential wire-pulling, lobbying and custom house politics. It has been intertwined with currency errors all the way along. It has created privileged classes in the free American community, who were saved from the risks and dangers of business to which the rest of us are liable. It has controlled the election of Congressmen, and put inferior men in office, whose inferiority has reacted upon the nation in worse and worse legislation. Just now we are undergoing a spasm of indignation at official corruption, and we want to reform the civil service, but there is only one way to accomplish that, and that is to cut up the whole system which has made the civil service what it is. It is of little use to cut off the tops of the weeds and leave the roots in the ground. When the shower passes over they will grow up stouter than ever.

I have presented the subject to you historically, because it is the method of treatment in which I have the most confidence. It is to history that we must look for the facts which teach us social and economic laws, and form the basis of any positive treatment of social questions. For a full exposition it would be necessary to follow the industrial history of the country, but the materials for such a history of this country are not in a shape to be available, if indeed they exist. We have enough, however, to show us that we are living here under immutable and inexorable laws of the social organization. We cannot cheat those laws, nor evade them. If we try to escape their operation in one point, they avenge themselves in another. We cannot manipulate the law of value, so as to make things exchange otherwise than in the ratio of supply and demand, without losing more one way than we gain another. We cannot legalize plunder under any guise whatever, without surely wasting wealth and impoverishing robbers and robbed together. We cannot arrange any system of gambling which will increase wealth, since wealth comes only from labor properly applied. We cannot employ the taxing power of the government to increase wealth, but only to diminish it. This is the world and human life as they are. The whole protectionist school, in its various grades, starts out with discontent with this world, and with *a priori* assumption in regard to the kind of world they would like to make. They are not contented to see what the natural chances of the country are and then to go to work to develop them. They make up their minds first what, in their wisdom, the country ought to be, and then they set to work to force it, with nature or against nature, into that form. They are not contented to see that the country affords by nature unexampled opportunities for man in agriculture and commerce. That is all as nothing if it cannot be one other thing also. They are not satisfied that it shall evidently be able to obtain all good things which the whole world produces by exchange, if not by production. They form to themselves dogmas about exchange, and will have nothing but by direct production, even though on the whole they have less. So they set to work to devise means to make the sort of country which they picture to themselves. We all sometimes grumble at the ills of life, I suppose; but I, for one, turn back from the study of all these propositions with devout thankfulness that we live in a world which God has made, and that these gentlemen may mar, but they cannot greatly alter it; and, looking back on our experience of what they have done for us, I think we may all submit gladly to things as they are in preference to the notions of Niles and Carey as to what they ought to be. This is a world in which toil is the road to wealth. It is a world in which industry, economy, prudence, temperance, are sure roads to health, wealth, comfort and happiness, if men will only leave those virtues to operate freely under the laws which are set for human life. It is a world in which idleness, extravagance, dissipation and want of thrift are sternly and piteously punished; unless men, by their laws, rob virtue of its rewards to transfer them to vice. That is all which any "protection" ever can do, and it is the worst injustice which law can perpetrate. It is the injustice of the old despotisms and caste aristocracies, and of all systems of class legislation and privilege, an injustice which has made history one long record of revolutions and social wars and broils and tumults. We may perpetrate it over again in the name of democracy, but we may be sure we shall only produce the same results. What is lacking in it is liberty, and in spite of the boasts of men about liberty, we are very far yet from understanding what it it. It is nothing but the removal of all restraints which hinder any individual from exercising all his powers under the best intelligence, to go towards happiness by the path of virtue which is laid down for us, but we may as well understand that it brings with it the chance that he may, blindly and ignorantly, choose the path of vice, which leads to ruin. When we plead for liberty we plead only that those of us who want to choose the course of prosperity and solid security may be left free to do so, or at least, that we may not be burdened in the attempt. When we ask for the liberty to exchange our products as we will, we ask only that, in that one particular, our efforts to advance ourselves may be left free to exert their full effect.

This brings us then face to face with the task which is at present incumbent upon us. We must have recourse to the means which are familiar to the habits of our people. We must organize societies and diffuse information. We must meet and discuss, and seek to gain and to propagate sound ideas. Our own welfare and that of our children depends upon it. If we are to have a fight, and we may expect that the whole cohort of selfish interests will make a strong stand for the control they have gained, we must meet it. The appeal lies to the great agricultural interest, which is the chief sufferer, and which numbers one-half of all the population of the country engaged in any occupation. The beginnings may be small and not very encouraging, but there is immense faith to be placed in sound and true doctrine when it is fairly and plainly taught, and it is impossible that a system of legislation so shameful and ignorant as our present tariff legislation can long disgrace a free country.

THE AMERICAN FREE TRADER---SUPPLEMENT.

NOVEMBER, 1882.
W. G. SUMNER.

PHILADELPHIA, PA., *October* 14, 1882.

Prof. W. G. SUMNER, of New Haven, Conn., addressed the Commissioners as follows:

I have noticed that in the discussions which have taken place before this Commission there has been a constant reiteration of some false doctrines of theoretical political economy about wages. If there is to be any theoretical political economy admitted, it is worthwhile to have it correct. I have therefore thought that it might be proper for me, as a professional student of political economy, to appear here and read a paper setting forth the true relations between protective taxes and wages.

I learn from the reports of the proceedings before this Commission that some people believe that protective taxes make wages high, and at the same time that high wages make protective taxes necessary. If the Commission should act on these two doctrines it would first raise taxes in order to raise wages in obedience to a delegation of workmen, and then raise taxes again in order to offset the previous increase, in the interest of a delegation of employers, and so on forever. These two notions, therefore, contradict each other, and produce an absurdity. They are both false. Protective taxes lower wages, and high wages are a reason for free trade, not for protection. These two propositions confirm and sustain each other, and so ratify the truth of each.

The interests of the man who pays wages and those of the man who receives wages are antagonistic. The one wants wages low and the other wants wages high. The protectionist legislator pretends to step in between them and satisfy both at once. He pretends to make both parties happy at once. "I am going to make your wages high," says he to the wage receiver. "What, then, will become of me?" says the wage payer. "I will make wages low for you," he replies. "How is that," cry the laborers and all their friends, "you are going to make wages low?" "No," replies the legislator, "I mean that I will make the price of the products high, which will have the same effect for the employer." "But how is that," cry the consumers, "you mean to make prices high by law?" "No," replies the legislator, "I do not really make prices high; it only looks so. My measures really make prices low." We have here, then, the greatest miracle that has ever been accomplished. We have heard of making something out of nothing, but here we have creation and destruction in one and the same act. Certainly the problem of universal happiness is solved if we have found out how those who buy need pay little, and those who sell may at the same time receive much; how prices may be raised for the producer and lowered for the consumer both at the same time. As we are all producers and all consumers, we may all sell at the high prices, and all buy at the low ones, and all get rich together. This is why it is that the protected manufacturers are found bulling what they are short of (that is, labor) and bearing what they are long of (that is, products). They have discovered this wonderful system by which all are to bull everything and bear everything at the same time, and win a big difference out of nothing. No wonder the protectionists are enraged at the economists who are still stupidly teaching that we can produce nothing except by applying labor and capital to land.

Who is the beneficent genie, now, who works all the magic of the protectionist system? It is tax. If taxes are only rightly adjusted, says the protectionist, they make wages high and low and prices high and low both at the same time. When one hears this kind of nonsense one is forced to believe that the sum of superstition in the world is a constant quantity. Superstition is a defective sense of causation. The savage who wears a bone tied to his arm as a fetich to ward off misfortune, believes that there is a connection of cause and effect where there is none. The astrologer thought that the relations of the planets to each other affected the fate of persons born at a certain time. He saw a connection of cause and effect where there is none. The protectionist legislator lays a tax and goes home secure in the faith that wages will be high, prices low, and prosperity stable, as if there were a fixed, direct, and inevitable law of nature connecting taxes with social welfare and nothing else. This superstition is more wild than fetichism or astrology.

In discussing the effects of taxation ambiguity is often introduced by not distinguishing carefully the alternatives which may be imagined. If we could imagine a state of society in which vice, passion, and other destructive forces no longer existed, government could be dispensed with, or it would sink into some low form of co-operation for common purposes. Taxes could then be dispensed with. If we compare our present condition with any such ideal state of things, all taxes are minus quantities, reducing by so much the available wealth and attainable comfort of the community. But such an ideal is a mere poetic dream. If we had no government we should have vice and passion running triumphantly through society, wasting and destroying on every side. Comparing our present condition with that state of things, the taxes which we pay for security, peace, and order as products of civil government are a small loss incurred to prevent a great one. Such is the only sensible and correct view of taxes. They are never anything but loss and diminution of wealth, and it is as impossible to convert them into productive forces as it would be to make destruction create, or waste save. Every tax is on the defensive, so to speak. It is necessary to justify every cent which is drawn from the community by taxes and to show that all the capital thus consumed is necessary, under the existing order of things, to secure the protection of society, on the cheapest terms, against the forces which would disturb security, peace, and order. If the taxes were large enough, they might, as in Egypt or Turkey, almost take the place of the evils against which governments pretend to guard society. Every unnecessary cent of taxation is, therefore, a pure evil. Government in Egypt and Turkey, and in much of Asia, is not an organization to defend society against evils. It is only an organization by which some plunder all the rest, and taxes are the means by which they do it. Wherever any taxes are laid for any other purpose than to provide civil order, peace, and security, government approaches by just so much towards the Turkish pattern. Such is the case whenever protective taxes are laid.

Taxes which ward off greater evils at the lowest practicable cost are economical. They do not lessen the average comfort of the people. Taxes which do not conform to this description do lower the average comfort of all classes of the people. The wages class has no separate interest in the matter which either can be or ought to be considered by itself. It is pure demagogism to say that it is the business of the government to make wages high. If I discuss the effect of taxes on wages, it is only by way of meeting the question in the form in which it is raised. Protective taxes do not aim to produce good government, or to accomplish any civil purpose at all. Their aim is industrial. They are planned to help some people to get a living. They interfere, on behalf of certain persons, with the conditions of production and the relations of competition. A man who engages in a protected industry has some other reliance in his business than his own capital, energy, enterprise, prudence, &c. The man who is in an unprotected industry has something more to guard against and contend with than the problems of his industry and the difficulties of the market. One of these parties has a special advantage created by law at the expense of the other party, who is therefore under a special disadvantage. These protective taxes, therefore, cannot be defended or justified under a sound view of the function and justifiability of taxation. They waste labor and capital, and keep the wealth of the country less than it might be for the labor and capital which have been expended. Let us examine in particular their effect on wages.

Anything which lessens the number of persons competing for wages, or which increases the amount of capital which may be divided in wages, increases wages. In a new country in which there is an immense amount of unoccupied land, and in which the amount of capital required for tilling the soil is small, any man who has a pair of stout hands, although he has no skill and very little capital, may become a land owner and agriculturist. He is then withdrawn from the wages class; he lessens the supply of labor in the labor market; and, as an independent producer, he contributes all the time to the capital of the country. Every man of the unskilled labor class, therefore, has an alternative offered to him. He is never driven by starvation into a desperate competition with others in the same predicament to work for low wages. He is on the right side of the market. Supply and demand are in his favor. He owns a thing for which there is a high demand in the market. The comfort he could win on the land fixes a minimum below which wages cannot fall. If they do temporarily fall below that minimum, the laborers take to the land, as they did in the hard times a few years ago. Since the comfort obtainable from an abundance of cheap and fertile land is high, the minimum of wages is high. This makes the average wages of the country high. High wages, therefore, simply mean that the soil of this continent is rich, the climate is excellent and well varied, the rivers are large and convenient, the mountains are full of metal and coal, the people are industrious and energetic and are eager to accumulate, the public order is fairly secure, and the general intelligence is good. The conditions of production are, therefore, good, and we produce a great deal. We accumulate capital far more rapidly than any other people in the world.

It is one of the humors of the tariff that the politician appears at this stage and says, "Oh, no! you are quite wrong in attributing the prosperity of the country to those causes. It was I who did it, with my little taxes. The country has prospered because I taxed it vigorously. If I had not put on my taxes the country would have been ruined." He argues that an industrious people on a fertile soil could not have got food and clothing out of it if they had not had the right taxes. A further touch of the ridiculous, however, is added by those politicians who declaim about the dignity of the American laborer. To listen to the speeches and read the editorials, one would think politicians formed a standard of comfort which they thought suitable for the American laborer and then just passed the right laws to get it for him. It is said that *our* laborers ought not to be on the standard of comfort of European paupers. It must be, then, that the American sovereign can formulate his demands on nature. He makes up his mind what is suitable to his own majesty, and serves notice on nature to provide it. His attorney, the politician, justly indignant that nature does not respond, passes a law to secure the becoming thing for his noble client, the American laborer. In this view of the matter, certain persons are "nature's noblemen" in a sense not heretofore used. A little examination shows us, however, that we are only dealing with an old fraud under a new face. The old-fashioned nobleman drew his drafts not on nature but on his fellow-citizens, and, as his friends were in control of the government, they got payment for him. The American sovereign can get nothing from nature which he does not earn. If the politician meddles in the matter he can only rob one sovereign to favor another. That is all that he ever has done. That process has never made us any richer, but only poorer.

Under the conditions of the United States, a tax on immigrants would probably lower wages, not raise them. The country is underpopulated. So long as there is an immense amount of unoccupied land the immigrants do not go to swell the wages class; they go upon the land, they open it up, win wealth from it, and contribute to the capital of the country. Each newcomer who is industrious, counts more as a pair of new hands to produce, than as another mouth to consume, and he may well add to the average wealth per head. Taxation has not even, therefore, in this country, the field which it might have in some countries, if it were used to keep competitors out of the labor market.

If a tax on laborers could not raise wages, certainly no tax on commodities can do so. Protective taxes aim to keep certain foreign commodities out of the country. An army of custom-house officers must therefore be supported, not to collect revenue, but to prevent revenue from being collected. This device is kept up in order to secure the home market to the home producer. The home producer carries on his business at a loss. He says that he would lose capital if it were not for the tariff. His industry, he says, would not exist if it were not for the tariff. It is therefore conducted at a loss all the time, only that the loss is not borne by the persons carrying on the business, but by the consumers of the goods. The protective system, therefore, involves the following expenditures: The pay of all the custom-house expenditures to keep up the system; wages and profits to all those who are carrying on the productive industries; the losses incurred by the protected industries. All these outgoes must be borne by the non-protected in order that there may be less goods of all kinds in the country than there might be under free trade. How, then, can protection increase wages, or the average amount of these goods which can be obtained by each laborer in the country? There could not be a more flagrant error. If there is anything cheap anywhere the protectionists spring into activity to keep the American people from getting it. If there is an abundance of food, clothing, furniture, and other supplies which is offered to the American people on easy terms, the protectionists call it an "inundation," and run to set a barrier against it. A few weeks ago I saw a hundred women waiting for hours on the sidewalk for the opening of a store at which some fire-damaged goods were to be sold cheap. A protectionist must hold that those women were insane, or that they were selfishly ruining the country. It is impossible to raise wages by opposing cheapness and abundance. The protective system lessens wealth and until somebody invents an arithmetic according to which 10 will go in 70 more times than it will in 100, it is certatain that smaller dividend will give a smaller share to each person. The protective system, therefore, lowers wages.

Let us next look at the effect of protective taxes on the alternative which is open to the American laborer to go upon the land. The protective taxes enhance the cost of all articles of clothing, furniture, crockery, utensils, tools, and machinery. They also increase the cost of fuel and transportation. They therefore reduce the amount of all the commodities mentioned which a farmer can get for a certain amount of farm products. They therefore lessen the profits of agriculture in all its forms, and lessen the attractiveness of the land. Whatever lessens the attractiveness of the land lowers the minimum gain of all manual laborers, increases the number of competitors in the labor market, and reduces the amount which the employer needs to bid in order to counteract the advantages of the land. Protective taxes, therefore, take away from the laborer the advantage which he has by nature in this country; that is to say, they take away from him part of his advantage in the labor market. Consequently, they lower wages.

It has been affirmed by protectionists that their system increases capital. Two ways have been alleged in which it does this, (1) by improving the organization of labor, (2) by bringing capital into use which would otherwise be idle.

1. The people of this country are all the time exercising their utmost ingenuity to organize their industry to the highest advantage. Partly they do this by instinct. Plenty of people never heard of the "organization of industry," but they are constantly arranging their business to save labor and so gain time and prevent waste. They are also constantly laboring intelligently to secure a better organization of industry. But, after they have exhausted their ingenuity, the protective system assumes that some other persons, viz, politicians and legislators, can see some better organization than the persons engaged in industry have themselves been able to devise. If one part of the American people have not invented the best organization of labor, we have no one else to call upon than some other portion of the American people, and we must appeal from the men of business to the politicians. The politicians, then, as an incident to their own occupations, rectify the errors and shortcomings of the business men. The mode they employ is taxes. It is the same old magic. But the business men have to bring intelligence to bear on the organization of labor, while the protectionist legislator never has brought any intelligence at all to bear on the problem, and he never can. Protective taxes have never been laid in view of any true knowledge of the industrial circumstances, and they never can be. A thousand commissions, sitting for ten years, and actually engaging in a real study of the industries of this country, could not win a knowledge of our industrial system, and if they could acquire such knowledge of the industrial system as it exists on a given day, their knowledge would not be good for anything the day after, on account of the new inventions, discoveries, processes, lines of transportation, financial arrangements, and so on.

We have here now fifty millions of people spread over a continent with great varieties of climate and soil, and we constitute the most energetic, restless, and indefatigable nation which has ever existed. To try to plan a system of artificial relations of industry for such a nation is the most ridiculous undertaking that could be proposed. Any one who talks of reaching a permanent adjustment of the tariff to fit the needs of all interests and do injustice to none is talking the wildest nonsense. Nothing less than the impersonal forces of nature can adjust interests under such conditions, and there is only one thing which can be predicated of any steps taken by the statesman, that is, that he will make mischief. A man who is running a railroad easily sees what crude nonsense people talk about railroading when they know nothing of the business. A banker makes the same observation. So does every other man in his own line. What chance is there, then, that politicians can deal wisely with the thousands of industries and interests in this country in all their manifold and complex relations to each other. We might as well try to establish, by legislation, a system of health which would prevent the people of the United States from ever being sick any more.

Furthermore, the politicians never try to deal with the whole combination of industrial interests. They listen only to the most clamorous. They heed only those who win influence and so secure the position of favorites. They never bring any intelligence to bear on the question. How much assistance is needed? There never is any adjustment of means to ends. No tests are ever applied; no guarantees are ever given; no subsequent reports are ever made by the recipients of favor to show results for the expenditure. Each interest comes forward and asks for favor and gets it for no reason save because it asked for it. The petitioner thinks that about so much per cent. will do and does not himself know or ever try to calculate what will be the effect of that much protection to him when offset by all the taxes to which he must submit in behalf of others in order that the system may be completed. Mr. Peter Cooper says that the tariff ought to just about offset the difference between American and European wages. If that could be done and were done, it would just take away from the American laborer those superior advantages which made him or his ancestors come across the ocean. Now, from this tangle of absurdities and contradictions, and ignorances, and guesses, it is expected that guidance will come which shall lead the American producer to a better organization of industry than he could arrive at if left alone, so that greater accommodation of capital and larger wages would follow. From such causes no result, save waste and loss, can ensue with reduction of capital and lowering of wages.

2. It is alleged, in the second place, that protection brings capital into use which would otherwise be idle. Every one of us who has any capital is anxious to put it to productive use without delay. It is impossible, in the nature of things, to keep all capital all the time employed. Improvements (such as a better credit system) which make this more fully realizable are eagerly adopted. The argument I have quoted means that in spite of this eagerness, and in spite of the chances for employing capital on a new continent, some portion of the capital now in protected industries would not be in use if it were not for protection. Such a notion is beneath discussion.

There is, then, no way in which protective taxes can produce capital. Every analysis shows that they waste it. Not a cent can come to A. by the action of the tariff which does not come from B. The consequence of universal borrowing or stealing or gift-making, however, is not to increase capital but to waste it. Hence protective taxes lower wages. The laborers have been exhorted to vote for protection lest their wages should be reduced to European rates. I have shown that the rate of wages obtained here is due to the economic forces at work in this country. There is only one thing which could reduce American wages to European standards, and that is protective taxes applied long enough and with sufficient weight.

There is, however, another argument which must be considered in this connection. It is said that under free trade all our population would go into agriculture, and that wages and all other remuneration for labor would be reduced until we should all be in proverty together. Hence the agriculturists, and the mechanical laborers, too, are exhorted to support a wide protective system in order to diversify industry and prevent ruinous competition.

We have seen above that the direct cost of keeping up the protective system consists of three items: (1) payment of custom-house officers to keep goods out; (2) support of laborers and profit on capital in protected industries; (3) the losses of the protected industries. These costs must be paid to buy off competition.

In the first place, it can pay no one to buy off competition unless he has a monopoly. Protected industries have done it sometimes. American farmers share the world's market with a number of strong competitors. If they buy off the competition of American manufacturers they must bear all the cost of it, and they must share the gain, if any, with all the agriculturists in the world. That means that if they try it they will put themselves at a great disadvantage with their own competitors in the world's market.

In the second place, all the protected industries of this country are now parasites on the naturally strong industries. Agriculture now supports itself and all the rest and all their losses. Therefore, even if it were true that all the population would, under free trade, take to agriculture, it is mathematically certain that agriculture could support them all better directly than under the present arrangement.

The farmers would indeed gain a great deal if the protected people would keep still and not do anything, for then they would at least waste nothing. The earnings of farmers and the wages of laborers would then not be reduced so much as they are now. The protectionist theory, however, is that it increases wages to keep on an occupation which wastes capital and lessens all the time the goods within reach of the population. It is interesting to apply this theory to some other cases.

On the protectionist theory it would be a means of raising wages to keep up a big standing army. All the soldiers would be withdrawn from competition in the labor market, and would consume while producing nothing. In time of peace they would not be destroying anything; but in time of war they would be just like a protected industry, they would be wasting capital all the time. In that case, then, they would raise wages all the more.

On the protectionist theory a leisure class of idle, rich people make wages higher than they would be if the same people should go to work. By the same reasoning women who now consume without producing would lower wages if they should go to work, and while consuming, as they now do, should compete in the labor market. Indeed this view of the matter is very often taken, and perhaps the popular view is that the rich make wages high, if they not only keep out of the labor market, but also consume luxuriously, and do not save anything.

On the protectionist argument paupers living in an almshouse raise wages as compared with what wages would be if the same persons should no longer consume unproductively, but should come out and compete in the labor market while consuming as before. On the same argument paupers who produce something, though less than they consume, lower wages compared with what would be the case if the paupers did nothing; still more as compared with the case in which the paupers should destroy.

On the protectionist argument, convicts in the State prison raise wages by consuming the product of taxation in idleness, and lower wages if they go to work, and while consuming as before, produce something, because in the latter case they compete in the labor market. In fact, criminals out of State prison would satisfy the protectionist reasoning still better. They always destroy far more than they produce, and they do not compete with laborers. They would, therefore, raise wages by their operations. It would be a limitation of their beneficent action to put them in prison as consumers in idleness, still more so to set them to work at a useful industry.

On the protectionist view of the matter the trade-unionists are right when they adopt wasteful processes, practice shiftlessness and neglect, study not to be skillful or effective, and try to make work, as they call it, believing that they thus raise wages. The protectionist and the trades-unionist both mistake toil for wages. They think that when they increase the difficulties which intervene between us men and goods they increase wages, and that to make goods abundant is to lower wages.

On the protectionist theory those men in the riot at Pittsburgh, who exulted in the destruction of the city because they thought that it would make work, which they confused with making wages, were right from their point of view. No man wants work; that is, toil, or irksome exertion. Least of all does the man who has no capital want toil. He supplies toil. He cannot supply and demand the same thing. He demands capital on which to live. When capital is destroyed and toil is necessary to reproduce it, the ratio in which toil must be given for capital is rendered more unfavorable to the laborer; that is, wages fall. If they do not fall on the spot where the destruction took place they must fall elsewhere whence the capital is drawn to replace the capital destroyed. If Pittsburgh had to be rebuilt other cities could be built up just so much less. If Pittsburgh had not been burned up the capital which went to replace it would have been used to employ laborers in adding so much more to the comfort and possessions of the country. The country is poorer for all time by the capital there destroyed, with all its accumulations. Just so every year that this nation, on account of the protective system, attains to the possession of a less amount of goods than it could have obtained under freedom, the effect is the same as if we had produced a city and had seen it burn up; and anybody who believes that the protective taxes raise wages must believe that to burn up cities raises wages. All these notions are miserable fallacies, which sin against the first elements of common sense. He who believes that the way to raise wages is to hinder people from getting at things easily and cheaply or to refrain from the most profitable modes of obtaining goods, must believe that workmen raise wages when they stop working and go out on strikes, and lower wages when they go to work again. Trades-unionism and protectionism are falsehoods. The way of prosperity for human society is by industry, economy, thrift, skill, energy, painstaking, excellence, liberty, abundance, and not by some crafty and artificial devices to produce scarcity and bad work. The protectionist system requires a new set of proverbs which have never yet found their way into any popular philosophy, such as these: Want makes wealth; destroy and prosper; taxes are wages; to have much produce little; blessed are the bad workman and the foolish capitalist, for they shall get abundance.

Let us now look at the other dogma: High wages make protective taxes necessary. It is the very opposite of the truth. If wages are high, that is the reason why no protective taxes are needed, even if they might be in some other case. In Germany the protectionists generally allege that lower wages in Germany than in England are a proof that Germany is industrially inferior and needs protection against England. The protectionist argument never flags on account of any little variation in the facts.

In the arguments under this head of the subject it is constantly assumed that wages are the controlling condition in production, or that there is some direct connection between the wages paid and the value of the product or the profits of the capitalist employer. These assumptions are false. Suppose that an individual comes forward and claims that he cannot compete because he pays higher wages than a foreign producer. When has any examination ever been made to find out whether such person has an adequate capital, or has a competent knowledge of the business, or diligently attends to his business, or has located his establishment wisely, or has organized his business economically, or has bought his raw material judiciously, or has kept up with improvements in machinery, or has not speculated with his product unsuccessfully, or has not violated some one of the other conditions of success? The wages paid are but one, and often one of the least important conditions of production. If it is alleged, as it constantly is in this controversy, in a sweeping way, that American industries need protection because American wages are higher than foreign wages, it is a case of joining a very wide inference to very inadequate premises. What are the comparative conditions of industry in America and elsewhere as regards convenience and cost of raw materials, quality and cost of machinery, rent of land used, character of the climate as affecting the requirements of various industries, national character as respects industry, diligence, sobriety, intelligence, &c., of labors, distance from the market or convenience and cost of transportation, convenience and cost of natural agents (coal or water), taxes and tax system, the security afforded by the excellence or otherwise of the government, &c.? Surely it is plain that these things are the conditions of production and the comparative money rates of wages, taken apart from the purchasing power of money, or the efficiency of labor, to say nothing of all the other conditions enumerated, are by no means a criterion for a decision whether an industry can be carried on successfully or not. The lists of comparative wages which have been made, and which are relied upon by protectionists, and are often accepted by free-traders as pertinent to the issue, and perhaps as decisive of it, have no value at all for the purpose. The employer alleges that he can make no profits because he pays high wages. He assumes, apparently, that wages and profits displace each other. It is certain that they do nothing of the kind. There is no ascertainable relation between wages and profits. Wages are paid out of the capital during the period of production. The employer tries to keep wages down, just as he tries to keep down cost and waste of raw material or wear of machinery, because he wants to economize on his outlay. He, of course, tries to minimize every outlay, because that is the road to success in the competition of the market, and to maximum profits. The price of his product when he gets it done will be determined by supply and demand on the market. He must replace his capital and then he will find out what profit he has. No law whatever can be established between this profit and the wages which were paid to the men while they were making the article. Profits and wages may both be high or both low at the same time, or one may be high and the other low. The fact is, that instead of one being displaced by the other they most always go together, both high or both low at the same time.

It is much more to the point to notice that profits are higher in this country than in Europe. We ought not to take too low views of human nature, but when an employer pretends to bull wages, we shall not believe him without examination. When we notice that profits are high in this country we can understand the applicants for tariff favors, without assuming any disinterestedness. No capitalist will go into a business which gives less profit than some other which is open to him. The American producer does not want to put up with the rates of profit which his European competitor is satisfied with. He wants the rate which he could get if he went into one of the industries which are favored by nature in this country. Instead of going where he could get it on a natural basis, he wants the law to tax his fellow-citizens to give it to him. The talk about wages is all for effect. It is only so much smoke and noise imported into the contest to obscure the issue. It has had no little effect, because no one has taken the trouble to expose it in detail. The competitor whom we fear most is England, in which country wages are higher than anywhere else in Europe. How does England pay high wages and beat all the others, if high wages are the controlling consideration? And if she pays higher wages than the continental countries and beats them all, because other considerations come in, why may we not pay higher wages than she and beat her, at least in our home market, because other considerations come in? The nearest approach to pauper laborers in Europe are agricultural laborers. Our farmers send their products, raised by men remunerated at American rates, and pay transportation, and beat the pauper laborers in their own home market. How can this be done if the criterion of possible competition is the comparative rate of wages?

If it is said that we cannot compete, what is meant? These phrases are allowed to pass without due examination. I cannot compete with my inferiors or with my superiors. I cannot compete with an Irish laborer at digging a ditch, and I could not compete with the late Mr. Scott in running a railroad. Could any taxes enable me to run a railroad as Mr. Scott did, and to earn such remuneration as he earned? Certainly not. No taxes can possibly enable a man to compete with a superior. Could any taxes enable me to compete with an Irish laborer at digging a ditch? Indeed they could. They might interfere between me and the laborer and prevent me from getting his services, and I might be forced to dig my own ditch, turning away from other and better paid occupations to give my time to an inferior occupation. That would impoverish me. Such is the only way in which protective taxes can make competition possible. They drive us down to compete with those who are far worse off than we instead of allowing us the full use of our natural advantages.

If we have high wages, then they are a proof of industrial superiority. They prove that there are some lines of industry open to us, as a nation, in which great returns for both labor and capital may be obtained. To argue from high wages that we need protection, is like arguing that a man needs charity because he is rich, or needs help because he is strong.

A true analysis of the facts therefore shows us that protective taxes lower wages, and that high wages are not a reason why protective taxes are necessary. We get the remuneration of labor by using our natural advantages. The remuneration of labor is high because the advantages are great. It will be highest if the laborer is let alone to use the advantages without any restraint or interference. If we get a high remuneration by the use of our advantages, our strength in competition will come from the very advantages of nature which gave the high rewards of industry. Thus every aspect of the matter is consistent and straightforward, clear and natural. The more we study the case in all its aspects, the more thoroughly is the free-trade solution of it confirmed, for, instead of entangling ourselves in ridiculous absurdities, we find that all the relations are simple and consistent.

The application of these ideas to the matter in hand is simple and direct. I have spoken wholly as a political economist whose business it is to study theoretical questions. If it is proper to do anything about wages, the right thing to do is to abolish all protective taxes, and that will let them rise where they ought to be.

By Commissioner KENNER:

Question. Of course you do not object to our receiving your communication (which I will admit is a very strong one, and probably as forcible as could be presented) under the well-known saying that "granting a logician his premises he can reach any conclusion he wishes"?—Answer. Yes; I object to that very much.

Q. You object to our taking your paper with that understanding?—A. Yes; I do, very much.

Q. Of course your long residence in New England has made you familiar with the soil and climate of that section of the country?—A. Yes, sir; I was brought up there.

Q. You recognize the fact that New England has attained a high position morally, intellectually, and financially?—A. Yes, sir; it is so understood, I believe.

Q. You recognize the fact, also, that the soil of New England, in fertility and in all other qualities which lead to great productiveness (I mean in reference to climate, &c.) cannot compare with the prairies of the West or the savannas of the South?—A. Yes, sir.

Q. Well, do you suppose that this great eminence which New England has attained, in its intellectual, moral, and financial condition, and in its immense accumulation of surplus wealth, could have been attained under a system of free trade; in other words, if there had been no tariff from the inception of the government down to the present day, do you think that New England could have attained that eminence and those qualities which constitute a great nation?—A. It is impossible to doubt it. It would have been much greater than it is now, if there had not been any tariff at all. The contrary hypothesis would force you to assume that the people of New England had been getting rich at the expense of the rest of the country, which I do not admit.

Q. You admit that they have got rich?—A. Yes, sir.

Q. And you admit the system under which they did get rich?—A. Yes, sir; they have borne up against obstacles.

Q. Have you visited the South during the last 25 years, or do you know enough of the condition of the South to answer such a question in regard to its present condition?—A. I have been in the South, but have not acquired any particular knowledge of that section.

Q. You have acquired such knowledge, I suppose, as you would get by looking at the landscape?—A. I was there a few days once, on political business; I did not go into the question of its industries at all.

Q. But you must have attained impressions from looking at the buildings and the landscape as presented to any person who travels through a country?—A. I had rather tell you just what was the fact. I went down from Louisville by the Jackson road to New Orleans and right back again, on an express train. So much as a man can see out of a car window in the daytime, I saw.

Q. Did you not see a directly opposite state of things from that which you have observed in any of the New England States?—A. Yes, sir; considerably.

Q. Did you not observe that the houses were in a dilapidated condition, and that the people were comparatively impoverished?—A. Yes, sir; that was the general appearance.

Q. And it formed a great contrast to the appearance of things in New England?—A. Yes, sir.

Q. Are you not aware that the system which you advocate has been adopted in the South for 50 years or longer?—A. No doubt. When I went down there they had just passed through a terrible war; their capital had been used up, and they were in the midst of a most horrible political muddle.

Q. I am glad to hear you admit the horrible political muddle. But the system which has been adopted by the Southern people is the one which you have been advocating here to-day; while the opposite system has been adopted by the New England States, by Ohio, Pennsylvania, and the Middle and Western States. They have taken advantage of this system which you say is all nonsense—the sublimest nonsense, utterly and ineffably ridiculous, and all that sort of thing.—A. I prove that it is.

Q. And I started out by saying that if you grant a logician his premises he can prove anything.—A. But I do not admit that in regard to my paper. We are not discussing logic. Besides, I do not think that is a good proposition in logic.

Q. We are not discussing logic, but, as a professor in a college, you cannot object to your statements being tested logically; as a matter of course you cannot object to that?—A. I do not want any logical dogmas interposed in the matter. I have no objection to a logical examination of my paper.

Q. I understand perfectly well. Our purpose is to arrive at the truth. We want to get at facts which will enable us to form some system of revenue which will be of benefit to the country. You appear before us to advocate a system, and I want to get at the bottom of that system in order to determine how far it will stand the test of fact as well as of theory. I suppose you will admit that it is the part of wise statesmanship to look at the results of a theory as well as to look at the theory itself as expounded by a logician?—A. No doubt you have to test theories; everybody admits that.

Q. Now we see one section of the country (and I have taken the South as an illustration; I speak of it without hesitation because I am a Southerner by birth, and have lived in the South all my life, so that my motives are not susceptible to being misinterpreted) in a very dilapidated condition. We have turned our backs on manufactures of every kind as a rule, and have adopted the theory propounded by Mr. Calhoun and other great men of the South, that we were tributary to the North, and have carried that theory into practice. The result has been that it has placed the South at the bottom of the hill, while New England and the Middle and Western States, such as Missouri, Illinois, Indiana, Kentucky, and Tennessee, which have adopted the opposite theory from the one adopted by the South, have reached, if not the top of the hill, at least a place very far up the slope. Now, as a commission appointed to prepare a system of revenue, or to revise a system which has been in existence for a long time, do you not think it wise on our part to look at the results of the two systems, instead of considering exclusively the theory of the one system or the other?—A. If you are going to discuss these results which you have alluded to, as shown by the present condition of the one section or the other of this country, you will have to go into the entire history of the country, not simply on the tariff question, but also in regard to the slavery question, the effects of the civil war, and everything else which has happened since the adoption of the Federal Constitution. Consequently, any deductions such as you suggest taking into account, with respect to Mr. Calhoun's theories of free trade, and the theory of protection, would certainly be very fallacious. It would be necessary to go over a great deal of ground to take the whole thing in. I have spent some time in the study of these questions, and could go into that matter if we had time.

Commissioner KENNER. No, I do not care to do that; that is not our business. We are appointed to investigate the question of revenue. If the question of slavery was before us I should be happy to hear you on that subject. although, probably, you would not be so happy to hear me.

The WITNESS. I should like to hear you on any subject.

Commissioner KENNER. If that question was before us, my views would be as plain and as practical, I hope, as they may be in regard to any other matter.

The WITNESS. I gave the only answer I could to your question, that the whole history of the country would have to be gone into to get at the causes of the results you speak of. But if you attribute the condition of the South solely to the effect of the tariff, you are wrong.

Q. But, as I have said, we have been appointed to prepare a system of revenue, and for this purpose we are endeavoring to collect the necessary information. You have suggested objections to the present tariff system. You have stated as facts certain things which other people deny. Whether you are right or they are right is a question for discussion between the two parties. But you have not yet told us what system you would recommend in the place of the present tariff. Suppose the present tariff was wiped out, and we were to follow your theory of letting labor seek its own market, and letting the products of labor be sold where they can be sold at the highest price, regardless of a tariff or any other outside consideration, what system would you advise us to adopt?—A. I am not a statesman at all; I cannot formulate a revenue system for the country. I have never taken such a matter upon me; it is quite out of my line.

Q. Our purpose is to get at the facts. I had supposed that when you condemned one system, you would be prepared to offer another to take its place.—A. I would say, give them all the free trade you can. Remove all protective taxes as fast as you can, or make them as low as you can, if you cannot abolish them altogether. That is all I have to say about it, speaking as a political economist. All protective taxes are mischievous, and you should get them out of the way if you can. If anybody tells you that a protective tariff raises wages, I come here to tell you that it does not, but that, on the contrary, it lowers wages.

Q. I do not think our purpose is to find out the way either to raise or to lower wages. Our object is to find out the best system of revenue.—A. Then abolish all protective taxes.

Q. Without regard to the $250,000,000 or $300,000,000, that it is necessary to raise for the support of the government? What would you recommend in the place of the present tariff system?—A. You have a large number of revenue taxes, and if you strike out half of them and divide the rest by two you would double the revenue, if you want more revenue.

Q. Divide which taxes by two?—A. All you have got—the whole tariff system, the whole intricate import tariff duties that we have. Strike half of them off the list and lower the rest to one half of what they are now and you will double the revenue.

Q. I thought you said just now that we should abolish all revenue taxes?—A. All protective taxes.

Q. All import duties?—A. I never said that; I said all protective taxes.

Q. I understood you to say abolish all protective taxes, and I understood you to mean by that all import duties.—A. Oh, no; I do not mean that.

Q. I wish you would be more explicit then.—A. I am as explicit as a man can be.

Q. I thought you considered all those duties as protective?—A. If you had a duty on tea, or on pepper, it would not be a protective tax; neither would a duty on coffee be a protective tax. If you have a duty on wine, that might be protective. The tax on sugar is largely a revenue tax, but it is also a protective tax on behalf of the Louisiana sugar growers. If you ask me what I want done, I say I want an excise put on Louisiana sugar men, in order to make them pay into the Treasury an amount equal to the protective tax; so that when I buy sugar I shall not pay any tax to the sugar grower at all. I want to pay taxes to the United States Treasury, but not to the iron man, the sugar man, the woolen man, or any other of my fellow citizens.

Q. I did not suppose that you proposed paying taxes to the United States Government. I understood you to be opposed to the present tariff system?—A. I oppose the protective system. Protective tariffs are the only ones I have discussed. I have not touched upon the revenue system at all. The minute you touch protection you touch what I am talking about. It is the business of Congressmen and statesmen to provide for a revenue, not the business of professors.

Q. What do you mean by a protective tax?—A. I mean a tax laid for the benefit of an industrial person in the country.

By Commissioner OLIVER:

Q. You mean a tax laid on any article produced in this country?—A. Yes, sir. It may be partly for revenue, and partly protective.

By Commissioner KENNER:

Q. You advocate a protective duty on articles not made in this country; and that the duty should be taken off all articles made in this country, agricultural, mechanical, and commercial.

The WITNESS. Please repeat that.

Commissioner KENNER. I asked you to define what you call a protective duty, and you say a protective duty is a duty imposed on any article grown or manufactured within the United States.

The WITNESS. No, sir; I did not say that. I said that a protective tax is one which is paid, not into the Treasury, but to some industrial person in the country. I would not object to paying a tax on iron, for instance, if the amount which I paid would go into the Treasury; but I do object to paying such a tax if it goes into the pockets of the Pennsylvania manufacturer. That is what I am opposed to, and nothing else. Such a tax favors the manufacturer in his business, and is not paid for revenue.

Q. Any duty which favors the business of the country is a protective tax which ought to be abolished; is that what you say?—A. Yes; I will say that, if it favors any particular business. It is not the object of taxes to favor the business of a country, not in the least. We must be on the lookout all the time for ambiguous terms in this discussion.

Q. There is another question I will ask, not because it affects you particularly, but because it affects everybody. I am an agriculturist by profession, and have been all my life; I am not a lawyer; and there is one point in this discussion which I do not understand. The manufacturer appears before us and seems to be enthusiastic in behalf of the interests of the poor man, and tells us that he wants a protective duty because it will protect the poor man and enable him to receive better wages. Now, on your part, are we to assume the same ground; that you want to protect the poor man?—A. No, sir; I do not make any such claim.

Q. Who, then, do you profess to plead for, or in whose favor do you make your statement if it is not in behalf of the mass of the community, and of those particularly who are not able to help themselves?—A. I speak for those who are now being oppressed and injured by existing legislation. I have stated the effect on them. As to favoring anybody, or coming forward to do anything more than to help a man stand on his own feet and look out for himself, I have not done it here, nor have I ever done it. I disclaim all that in my paper and do not make any such special plea. I think it is the business of demagogues to do that. It is not the business of the government to make wages high or to favor the poor laboring man, except to let him do the best he can for himself. I make a plea against protective taxes because they keep these men down; because those who receive small wages have to pay their share of the public loss that the protective system inflicts on the country.

Q. As I have said, our object is to formulate a proper revenue system; that is our duty, and if you can suggest such a system we shall be glad to receive such information. Have you done that in your paper?—A. No, sir; I have not. I have only talked about the relation of protective taxes to wages; I have not undertaken to talk about a revenue system.

Commissioner BOTELER. I have listened with great interest to your paper and to your answers to Commissioner Kenner. You have announced yourself as a political economist, as a theorist, and as we are practical men with a practical object in view, I should be glad, for my part, to have you answer the question, in the first place, whether England is not confessedly more perfect in her industrial pursuits, and has not made more industrial progress than any other nation of the world?

The WITNESS. Yes, sir; in some lines.

Q. In all lines of manufacturing industry, I mean?—A. No, sir; not in all lines.

Q. Well, except in those manufactures, perhaps, that require nicer manipulation with respect to some minor matter, such as the French make a specialty of?—A. The Germans are ahead of them, I think.

Q. Will you please tell me how you can reconcile your theory, as announced in your paper (which I consider as very forcibly expressed), with the fact of England's progress: to what is her commercial pre-eminence to be attributed?—A. In the first place, to the fact that she had the richest stores of coal and iron that existed anywhere in the world.

Q. How did she come to make them valuable; did she not protect her industries for more than two hundred years?—A. I was wondering which particular erroneous view of English history you might have in mind.

Q. Beginning with the time she introduced through the Flemings the wool industries that have made her so great, has she not given the most rigid protection to all her industries?—A. Yes, sir; for awhile she did, very much to the injury of all her industries, and which has set her back a century, perhaps.

Q. Inasmuch as she has commanded a great share of the commerce of the world as an exporting nation, should we not in some degree attribute her success to her protective system?—A. Not at all. The protective system was never anything but a great injury to her, and there is hardly a writer now who does not take that view.

Q. To what is her great prosperity attributable, then?—A. To the extraordinary natural advantages which she possessed, especially in having a great store of coal and iron available and close to each other, and to the extraordinary energy and industry of her population. When you consider these things you get at the secret of her success.

Q. We have as many natural advantages and resources as any country in the world. Do you think we should have attained any great degree of eminence in the production of those manufactured articles that have made us important in the world's history, if we had been kept in subjection to England and received our supplies from the old country instead of improving our natural advantages?—A. The colonial system was nothing in the world but a protective system.

Q. It was a protective system to England, but not to us. It did not encourage manufactures here; on the contrary it restricted them. So far as the protective system existed in the old country it had no application to our country?—A. Yes, it did. It was exactly the same as the levying of taxes on the Western farmers to-day for the benefit of the Eastern manufacturers—identically the same. The application of the colonial system of Great Britain to the colonies did not differ by a hair from the protective system of to-day. I am a pretty careful student of all these matters, and I think I speak with all the facts behind me. If you gentlemen would learn the theory of the matter—

Commissioner BOTELER. We are practical men, and want only facts.

The WITNESS. I suppose you understand that a man who speaks where he knows his reputation is at stake has to have his proofs behind him. The limitation on the industries of these colonies was a sacrifice of their interests to the interests of Great Britain; and the protective system to-day as it exists in the United States is a sacrifice of the interests of the Western farmer to the interests of the Eastern manufacturer. That is where the peril is. You can study it as closely as you like and look into the matter as far as you can, but you cannot get away from that.

Commissioner BOTELER. We have traveled many thousand miles during the last few weeks, searching for facts, in the humble hope that we might be able to send to Congress a record that would be considered as a mirror of the public sentiment of the country, and we have never yet found in the neighborhood of any manufacturing town where the farmer finds a ready market for his perishable products, one single person who did not rejoice in the establishment of such manufactories and feel that the greatest encouragement that could be given to the farming community was to vary the industries of his region of country and develop a market for his products.

The WITNESS. That is the famous truck-farm argument.

Commissioner BOTELER. Still, I am happy to tell you that we find a great many of those truck-farms springing up in a section of country which has heretofore neglected manufactures. We find a great change of public sentiment in those localities. While we may find free-trade theories obtaining in New England, emanating from the colleges of Massachusetts and Connecticut, we were glad to find that the people are a long way ahead of the politicians in the South, and are bringing these matters home practically, and applying them to their own business, and are proclaiming themselves as earnestly and honestly in favor of a protective tariff.

The WITNESS. I know these fallacies are very strong, indeed, and if a man gets them into his head it takes a long time before he can get them out.

The PRESIDENT. Whatever difference of opinion may exist between Professor Sumner and myself, he has stated his case so clearly and with such perfect distinctness that no question of mine could bring out his views more completely; and as I do not regard it as 'our province to talk, but simply to listen, I do not desire to put any questions to him.

By Commissioner MCMAHON:

Q. I understood Professor Sumner to reply, in answer to a question, that a tariff for revenue would necessarily be, in some degree, a protective tariff. [To the witness:] Do I state your position correctly?—A. No, sir. Revenue and protection are entirely exclusive of each other, and never can overlap one another at all. The minute you touch protection you prevent revenue, or, to put it in a simpler form, if I buy a ton of imported iron, it comes though the custom-house and I pay an import tax to the government for it. On the other hand, if I buy the iron in this country I pay an equivalent tax to the iron producer here, but do not pay anything into the United States Treasury.

Q. I understood that part of your answer, but there was another subdivision of it which I did not understand. Do you mean to say that where a tariff is placed upon an article that is not produced or manufactured in the United States (such as tea and coffee, for example), there can be no protection?—A. No, sir; no protection on that.

Q. But whenever an import tax is placed upon an article which is produced in the United States, that then it is protection?—A. Yes, sir; unless it is offset by an excise, as in the case of tobacco, wine, and cigars.

Q. Then I understand that your theory results in this: that if an article is produced or manufactured in the United States the producer or manufacturer of that article is protected to the extent of that tax unless that article is offset by an internal-revenue tax or excise?—A. Yes, sir.

Q. Then I understand your second proposition to be that the agriculturists of the country—the farmers—have to pay this protective tax to the manufacturers?—A. Yes, sir.

Q. Do the manufacturers have to pay any protective tax to the farmer?—A. No, sir; they pay to each other, all round, but not to the farmer.

Q. You say that the agriculturist pays a tax to the manufacturer whenever he buys a manufactured article?—A. Yes, sir.

Q. But when the manufacturer buys a produced article which is taxed he does not pay anything to the farmer?—A. On the agricultural product? No, unless you call sugar an agricultural product (which, of course, it is), or hemp, but not on wheat.

Q. Why not on wheat?—A. Because there is a tax on wheat in the tariff. Of course it is ineffective, because the producers of this country are exporters. I understand, however, they have been getting wheat from Manitoba lately, and they have had to pay this tax.

Q. Then does not the manufacturer pay that tax?—A. The mill-owner pays that, and then it comes to the manufacturer, who consumes it. But when the wheat comes from Manitoba to this country, where the production of wheat is 500,000,000 bushels, although technically it is a protective tariff, it does not amount to much.

Q. It theoretically exists in the other case. Suppose we do not import certain articles of manufacture, still we are paying the tax on them under your theory. The agriculturist is paying that tax to the manufacturer, although there is no importation of those articles?—A. There you would have to take each fact by itself. It would be a matter of statistical inquiry to see how much there was imported and where it goes. You could not generalize upon that. Take this matter of wheat imported from Manitoba, and that is a protective tax for the agriculturist right along there on the border.

Q. Here are some generally conceded facts, I believe. We do not import any beef or pork. We do import ham and bacon. We import a considerable amount of foreign ham because it is supposed to be better in some respects than ours. Is not the duty on those articles a tax on the manufacturer? We also have imported potatoes and other vegetables of late, although we raise them in this country; is not the duty on them a tax on the manufacturer?—A. Yes, sir; that would be like sugar, and there is unquestionably a protective tax on rice—a very unjust one. There are, of course, a number of agricultural products on the tariff list.

Q. And a considerable importation of them?—A. There are importations under several heads unquestionably, and it makes it appear to the agriculturist as though he was getting something back once in a while; but he pays $100 and gets one cent in return.

Q. We have developed, in the course of our investigations, the fact that we have imported for some years more barley than we have exported?—A. Yes, sir; a great deal of barley has come in from Canada.

Q. Was not that a large tax on the manufacturer?—A. No doubt that would be a set-back towards the agriculturist, of that particular article.

Commissioner McMAHON. That is all I desire to ask. You had spoken particularly of the agriculturist as alone paying the tax.

The WITNESS. The agricultural interest of this country bears the expenditure that is involved by the tariff in regard to manufactures. You cannot get something out of nothing. If you get a cent for a manufacture, by means of the tariff, that you could get in no other way, it has to come out of somebody, and in the end it is the agriculturist who pays it, as he is engaged in a fundamental industry. He is strong and independent, and he has got to pay it all. As to the manufacturers themselves, they are all the time scalping one another, and, therefore, I do not believe they make anything out of it. I believe it is all a great folly, from the standard of the manufacturer. If all the manufacturers of this country could be dropped right down on a free-trade basis, with all their supplies free, and their raw materials free, and if their workmen could buy their shoes, hats, clothes, crockery, furniture, stoves, bedding, and all the rest of it, on a free basis, they would all find themselves far better off than they are to-day. If, instead of trying to scalp each other, they would begin on a free-trade basis and get down to hard pan they would be far better off, and there would be an immense saving of waste—the cost in keeping up the system as it exists to-day.

Commissioner KENNER. That is the doctrine that has been advocated in the South for the last fifty or sixty years.

The WITNESS. And I hope they will stick to it.

Commissioner KENNER. They will not stick to it; they have seen the folly of it.

The WITNESS. They are going to begin to manufacture there to their very great loss.

Commissioner OLIVER. To their loss, or New England's loss?

The WITNESS. New England can stand it. I do not think it would be any loss to the country if there was no New England.

Commissioner KENNER. I agree with you in that last remark; that it would be no loss to the country.

The WITNESS. And it would be no harm to the country if there was no Louisiana.

Commissioner KENNER. Yes; there would be. I wish you would prove that proposition. We tried to leave the country and you would not let us, and yet you say it would be no loss. That is a *non sequitur* which I do not understand.

The WITNESS. We should all live here and be happy and get our living, even if there wasn't any New England, any Louisiana, or any Pennsylvania, I suppose.

Commissioner OLIVER. The Commission is composed of practical men, and we have been endeavoring for the last three months to try and learn as much about these matters as possible. We have visited all sections of the country and have examined the subject in all its various forms. The views of a gentleman of your standing, who occupies the position which you do in one of the largest and best-known institutions of learning in the country, where we send our children to be educated, are entitled to respectful consideration; but when you make such very radical suggestions as you have made, we want to see how far you can substantiate them.

The WITNESS. By all means.

Q. I have only a question or two to ask you. I suppose you will admit that large numbers of Irishmen come to this country every year and are successful in business. Is there a more purely agricultural country in the world than Ireland?—A. No, sir.

Q. Is there a country in the world, with the same population, which has fewer manufactories?—A. They manufacture but little in Ireland.

Q. I understand from your argument that you are opposed, for example, to having help extended by the government, directly or indirectly, in the establishment of steel-rail factories. You think that industry should have waited its proper time of development and not have received the benefit of a protective tax, or any help in the way of extra prices?—A. Yes.

Q. Do you think that argument would apply to every industry, or to every institution?—A. Do not let us use the word "institution"; let us say "industry."

Q. Very well; we will say industry. An institution may be connected with an industry. You are connected with an institution which has attained great eminence, and to which the sons of our leading men are sent for instruction. Do you think your college would have attained that position but for a protective tax, as it might be called? I mean the benefit it has received in the way of legacies left to it by rich men at different times.

The WITNESS. Is that a protective tax?

Commissioner OLIVER. I do not know. I just ask you the plain question whether you would have attained the position which you have attained as an industry, without such assistance?

The WITNESS. We are not an industry. We are sinking capital all the time.

Commissioner OLIVER. I know you are, and that is the reason why I ask you the question.

The WITNESS. Certainly, we have a small endowment, but it is very insignificant, and we really earn what we get. The endowments of Yale College do not amount to more than fixed capital, and we have to earn all we get; if we did not we should soon stop. But still, admitting that an institution may be well endowed, it would not have any comparison with a protective tax or anything of that sort, any more than an endowment to an insane asylum would.

Q. Would it ever be able to stand on its own footing, without such extra help?—A. It does now, by earning what it spends. But, of course, no educational institution in the world could support itself unless it was a private school.

Commissioner OLIVER. I was trying simply to call your attention to the fact that while it is necessary to have colleges, yet they need protection.

The WITNESS. No, sir. In a sense, it was not necessary to have them here; they made themselves. I cannot admit that they have anything at all to do with the protective theory we are talking about. I cannot see the slightest or remotest connection.

By Commissioner MCMAHON:

Q. I understand you to say that you do not believe in favoring any one person, or class of persons, at the expense of any other.—A. No; not at all.

Q. Then, inasmuch as the present tariff admits free of duty for schools and institutions of learning, like the one you are connected with, many articles, such as books, maps, charts, philosophical and scientific apparatus, and chemical apparatus, by special exemption, you would be in favor of an imposition of a duty on all such articles?—A. Not at all; that only means that Congress has relieved the great institutions of the country of a little bit of the iniquity involved in this system. They have not relieved me of it personally. I have a great personal grievance in regard to books. I am a poor man, living on a small salary, and working hard for it. I want all the books I can get from my toil; but when I go to buy them I find the law of my country has got in my way and says that I cannot have those books until I pay an extra price for them, which is not necessary. I ought to be able to get all the books I need on the business basis of supply and demand, at a certain price; but the law says I must spend a part of my small salary in order that certain great American publishers shall be protected.

Q. Do you think it is fair, then, for such an institution, which pays you so small a salary, to get these articles in free of duty?—A. I am glad that they can get out of paying it; that somebody can get out of paying it. I do not want all the world crushed by such iniquity, because I am exempted from it. I am glad if there is any let up on it, and I wish there was more.

By Commissioner OLIVER:

Q. Your argument, at the outset, was that protection does not benefit the laborer.—A. That protection lowers wages.

Q. Now I will take an illustration on that point, which has occurred to me. The material to make a ton of pig iron within 50 miles of this city is not worth over 50 cents or $1 a ton—I mean the ore, coal, and limestone in the hill. Everything else necessary to make that ton of pig iron is the labor, is it not?—A. Very likely; I do not know the details of the industry; but I dare say it is.

Q. The cost is in the labor and transportation, and transportation is labor. The price of a ton of pig iron of equal quality in England today would be about $11 or $12 a ton, while the price here would be about $22 to $23 a ton. Now, how can you maintain your argument, when the same quantity and amount of labor in Eastern Pennsylvania is worth $22, and in the Cleveland district in England it is only worth $11, one under free trade and the other under protection?—A. That is exactly what is wrong about it. It does not make any difference what the wages are over there.

Q. There the laborer gets 50 cents a day, and here he gets $1.25 a day?—A. That does not make any difference.

Q. It makes a difference in his style of living, and a difference in the condition of the man's family who receives $1.25 a day instead of 50 cents a day, doesn't it?—A. Not at all; the only difference is whether he can make $1.25 in making iron easier than he can in tilling the land. You cannot cut him down to 50 cents a day wages, because the laborer in Europe receives that; or to 10 cents a day wages, because the laborer in China receives that. You cannot get the American laborer down below the American rate. The iron manufacturer wants protection because he cannot get the American laborer to work below the American rate, and he will not work in iron unless he can do better than in something else. Because a man gets 50 cents a day in England for doing that work does not affect the case.

Q. Is it not that the reason why the laborers are leaving Ireland, Germany, and other countries, and coming here?—A. Certainly; they say, "We will go to America and make iron and get as good wages as if we were tilling the ground." But it does not come out of what they make; they do not produce it. It comes out of me and the other consumers; and that is what we are growling about.

By Commissioner MCMAHON:

Q. They would not come to this country except for the difference in wages, would they?—A. They would if they wanted to. They will come if they can find profit in it; if not, they will stay at home. They are coming fast enough now, whether they find profit in it or not. Let us stand off and let them do as they like, if they are not living off of us. If they are to live off of our people, the more that come the worse for us. When I see a ship-load of immigrants landed on our docks, I feel anxiety, because I know that we shall have to pay more taxes to help support them.

By Commissioner KENNER:

Q. Then you object to immigration?—A. No, sir; not at all.

Q. I understood you to say so; it seems I cannot understand you at all?—A. The trouble is that you do not get my idea of labor: that I do not want to prescribe what any man under God's heaven shall do. Let every man stand on his own basis and help himself. I do not want to be taxed to help support him.

Q. But you do not want him to remain in ignorance?—A. Every man has to take care of himself and win his own way through the world, as I have had to do and as all the rest of us have had to do.

YALE COLLEGE
LOAN LIBRARY
of Political-Economy.

November, 1879.

BIMETALLISM.

IT has been made a ground of reproach against the professional economists that they have not exerted themselves sufficiently to expose the fallacies of bimetallism, but have been contented to pass it by in contempt. Especial point has been given to this reproach by the observation that a great many persons have only resisted bimetallism by a kind of sound instinct. This instinct does not furnish rational ground for conviction, and many such persons have therefore either wavered or been disturbed in their allegiance to sound doctrine. It belongs to the scientific economists, it is said, to show, upon due analysis of the question, wherein the fallacy lies, and to give rational grounds for sound doctrine.

It is not worth while to mention the reasons or the excuses for the neglect to which this complaint refers. If an economist should undertake to expose and combat all the fallacies which gain more or less acceptance, he would not have time for anything else. In the present instance there are more narrow and peculiar difficulties. If one attempts to refute the whole silver doctrine in all its forms, one must demonstrate a sweeping and general negative. If one attempts to select and refute a single form of the error, he will find that no writer on that side of the subject has stated his opinions and doctrines in a form upon which issues can be joined, and a scientific discussion carried on with any prospect of satisfactory results. He will be compelled to argue both sides at once, to put the adversary's case in shape for him before discussing it, and, if he attempts this, he is sure to be entangled in endless charges of misrepresentation and misapprehension. For instance, one writer adopted the term "concurrent circulation," and gave it frequent and current use to express his doctrine and aim. I thought the term well chosen to express the writer's idea as I understood it, and it seemed to me that here was an idea so clear and precise that we could join issue upon it, make an analysis, undertake verification, and so refute or demonstrate, which is what I understand by discussion, and not the heaping together of statistics, historical facts, and authorities. In a later publication, however, the same writer says: "The concurrent use of the two metals, side by side, in the same market is a matter wholly of indifference." We have then this proposition: The bimetallists want a concurrent circulation, but it is matter of indifference whether it be concurrent. There is here, then, no proposition to discuss, but only an illustration of the vague and loose thinking upon which the whole notion of the bimetallists is constructed.[1]

I. What I propose now to treat is bimetallism as it is popularly, however vaguely, believed in in the United States, as it is partially adopted in our legislation, and as it was expressed in the Act under which the Silver Commission was sent to Paris. The appearance of the Report of this Commission[2] furnishes the occasion and the means for examining this notion.

It was provided in the Act known as the Silver Bill that the President should invite the governments of other nations to join in a conference "to adopt a common ratio between gold and silver, for the purpose of establishing internationally the use of bimetallic money, and securing a fixity of the relative value between those metals." The legislators who enacted this assumed and believed that there was no impossibility, in the nature of things, in uniting two metals in the circulation at a fixed ratio of value; they believed that, this plan being debarred by no natural impossibility or absurdity, its expediency could be resolved upon in a conference, and that the means by which it could be realized was an international agreement of the chief commercial nations. I understand that these opinions are held more or less distinctly by all those who are popularly called silver men amongst us. I take issue upon both the points involved.

[1] Mr. Horton uses the term "concurrent circulation" constantly in his essay appended to the Report mentioned below.
[2] Senate Executive Document No. 58, Forty-fifth Congress, Third Session. References to "Report" refer to this document.

1. The first raises a scientific question: Is the notion that two metals can be joined in the coinage at a fixed ratio, by any human device or artifice whatever, true in science? I answer, No; it is just as false as the proposition, A perpetual motion is possible, would be in mechanics. This is certainly the first issue to be settled in regard to the silver controversy as between educated men; but the bimetallists have always slurred it over. At Paris, Count Rusconi did indeed recognize the primary importance of this question in the first session, but much contempt was expressed for the "academic" question, and there was great eagerness to be "practical" and to go on to the "practical" question. This is, indeed, the course of the "practical men," so called. They are impatient of the dogmatism of the professors, who say a perpetual motion is impossible, and insist on going on to consider the great practical advantages which would accrue *if* a perpetual motion were possible, and then, because they think they see such advantages, they go to work to construct the machine. The answer is, that if a perpetual motion, or a bimetallic circulation, were possible, this would not be the same world it is now. It might be a better one, but surely any practical man, in the correct sense of the word, will inquire whether there is any insuperable obstacle, in the nature of things, to the object he wishes to accomplish, before wasting his time upon it. If this is not so, what we call education is a pure waste of time. I had supposed that it was understood and agreed, amongst educated men, that the chief end of studying the sciences was to acquire that training by virtue of which we recognize the relations of man to nature, and the limits of human action.

The inference to be drawn from the importance and true position of the scientific question is not that that question ought to have been discussed in the Conference. Far from it. That was no place for such a discussion. The inference is that the Conference was *ab initio* an absurd and senseless undertaking. The requisite antecedents of any joint action of nations are, (1) that all scientific questions involved shall have been maturely discussed by scientific men until a substantial unanimity of conviction has been reached as to what is true; (2) that these convictions shall have been dogmatically taught in books and periodicals until they have become interwoven with the stock of convictions and faiths of the mass of civilized men; (3) that general opinions as to what it is expedient to do should, by necessary inference, have come to be held by all civilized men. When these conditions are fulfilled it is, of course, found that, for almost all cases, private contract, custom, or the independent legislation of individual states, concurring because proceeding from commonly accepted principles, answers all the purpose. The field for international conventions has therefore hitherto been restricted to postal conventions (common regulations for conducting a form of business which is monopolized by governments, but in which they act like the managers of any other business), or conventions on points of international law (in which the aim is to do justice to humanitarian sentiments wnich have become universal). The difficulty of these latter conventions, even, is instructive for the nature and limits of international conventions, and the history of the Latin Union, as an isolated effort towards international action for other purposes, is certainly a warning and not an encouraging precedent. When, however, the action proposed involves scientific truth, and yet all the necessary conditions precedent are passed over unfulfilled, the proceeding is devoid of sense. It could only have the form of sense if the object were to supersede scientific discussion by action and force—the fallacy of the ecclesiastical councils. The scientific question belongs where I now undertake it: in the forum of academic discussion.

We have then one issue joined; I propose to show that a bimetallic circulation is as absurd and impossible as perpetual motion, so that a convention of the whole human race could not realize it.

2. The second assumption in the Act above quoted relates not to a scientific truth, but to a point of expediency and practicability. It is assumed that an international coinage union, combining and binding the members to a certain programme of action, is a practicable scheme, and needs only a certain degree of consultation to be realized. I shall maintain that such a coinage union is absolutely impracticable. The bearing of this is not directly upon bimetallism, for that is disposed of when it is shown to be absurd, but the coinage union is an element in the

scheme properly known as the alternate or alternative standard. These two schemes, when tested and weighed from the scientific standpoint, are of totally different character and value, as I shall show further on. The question about the alternate standard is a question of expediency and practicability in the main, although it also involves considerations of rights and justice. The difference is that between a perpetual-motion machine and an ordinary machine invented to meet a certain purpose. As to the latter, the questions may be raised whether it will work so as to do what it is made to do, whether it will pay, whether it is dangerous, etc., but if one or all of these questions were decided adversely to the machine, it would still not be an abomination in mechanics like a pretended perpetual motion. The parallel holds in the case before us. The alternate standard is inexpedient for a variety of reasons, and it is impracticable because it involves the necessity of an international coinage union, prescribing regulations and dictating action to its members, and such a union is impracticable. Still the alternate standard involves no scientific absurdity. I therefore join issue, secondly, on the question of the practicability of the coinage union.

II. Before entering upon the subject-matter, a word of explanation is necessary on a certain point. If a monometallist means a man who urges that all nations ought to use gold money, I know of no such person in the world. It is one great error of the bimetallists that they assume to know and judge what money all the world ought to use. No one can reach any such judgment, on the one side or the other, who uses correct processes in the investigation of economic truth. Every nation ought to use just that money which, in its own judgment, its interests and convenience dictate. The economist has to note what course nations pursue under this motive, to study the consequences, interpret the phenomena, and deduce the inferences which are presented to him by the facts themselves. For myself, therefore, I have always repudiated the name Monometallist as a sectarian name, which no scientific economist would be willing to bear.

III. The historical facts bearing on bimetallism and kindred topics have been collected with great zeal during the last few years, but they have rarely been interpreted with the simple fidelity and loyalty just described. Let us recapitulate as briefly as possible, in their chronological order, the facts which are here of importance.

A. The attempt to use two metals together has been kept up from the earliest use of money to the present time, and has constituted a problem in money. It was deemed necessary to use two metals, but no means has ever been devised for using two which has not failed, besides producing confusion, loss, injustice, and commercial distress. In 1717, still essaying to solve the same problem, the English guinea was rated at 21 silver shillings. It was not worth that amount, and so became the cheaper medium, and the standard of prices and credits. The good silver coins were melted, and those which remained were clipped so as to be worth less than $\frac{1}{21}$ of a guinea. After the clipping once began, it went on from worse to worse, as always under the same circumstances, but the need for "change" kept the silver coins afloat. After the middle of the century the depreciation became so great that it led to a clipping of the gold coins also. In 1773 silver coins were made legal tender for no sums over £25, by weight, at 5s. 2d. per oz. In 1785 France adopted the ratio of 1 to $15\frac{1}{2}$ in a reformation of the coinage, as another attempt to hit the true ratio and keep the two metals in circulation. In 1803 the same ratio was ratified. The French law of 1785–1803 was therefore no new or special solution of the coinage problem, but only another attempt such as those which had been made before. Under the operation of this law, France used silver as a standard until the middle of the century. In 1816 a new coinage system was adopted in England which really accepted and put into a system the state of things which had grown up by custom during the last century—single gold standard, with silver subsidiary depreciated coins, limited in amount, and limited legal tender. It was from a study of the phenomena produced during the previous century by the operation of the laws of trade upon the legal system that the English statesmen were led to this system. The law, therefore, followed custom and the laws of trade, and did not attempt to coerce them. The sovereign now became a money of moneys, i.e., other moneys and currencies were common denominators of value within certain local limits. When a second common denominator was wanted to connect the operations of these local areas with each other, the sovereign met the need. That English money and English commerce thus mutually sustained each other was only an illustration of the principle that good institutions support prosperity and prosperity supports the utility of good institutions. The connection between them is organic, not mechanical. In 1834 the United States passed a new law for a coinage of two metals, but purposely rated the metals so as to get gold. In 1853, having obtained a gold standard by the operation of the law of 1834, they reduced all the silver coins except the dollar to a subsidiary condition, and introduced the English system. In 1853-4, by the fall in gold, France, under the operation of her law, became a gold country. She was burdened with the expense of the change from silver to gold, but this was regarded as a slight price to pay for a change which was opportune to her interests. In 1865 the Latin Union was formed. The nations composing it adopted the French law, and became like France, by the operation of that law, gold countries. In 1867 an International Monetary Conference was held, at which it was proposed to establish, by agreement, what existed in fact—the use of gold as a standard amongst the nations represented. After the formation of the North German Confederation in 1867, an event which to a certain extent met the German aspirations for political unity and national standing, it was felt that one of the greatest obstacles to the realization of the further hopes of commercial and industrial greatness lay in the currency of the country. The standard was silver. The coins were cumbersome. The small coin was, much of it, base billon. The bank-note currency also required reformation. After the war of 1870 and the formation of the empire, all the motives for a currency reform were increased in force, and when such reform was undertaken, all the considerations which had weight dictated that it should be carried through to the adoption of the gold standard. The Scandinavian nations followed the example of Germany. In 1873 the United States codified and simplified their coinage laws according to the existing laws and customs of the country, and according to what would best serve the interests of the country when specie payments should be resumed. They struck the silver dollar from the list of coins which the mint was permitted to coin, on which list it had stood as an idle and unused permission, and brought the United States to the simple gold standard with subsidiary silver. In 1873 silver began to fall by important steps. The operation of the French law would now have taken away gold and given silver to the Latin Union. The movement in this direction, however, was far differently welcomed from the contrary movement of 1853. The Latin Union refused to give up a gold currency and take silver, and undergo the loss of sustaining silver besides. It closed its mints against silver, and the "double standard" ceased to be.

1. Any one now who reviews this series of historical facts, not in order to interpret them by some ulterior design assumed to have existed,[1] but for just what they are, will see that there was no ulterior design, no set purpose, no agreement or combination, but that each nation acted as its own interests dictated, and that the concord of action and general tendency towards the adoption of gold on the part of all the great commercial nations, substantially in the order of their commercial importance, constitutes one of those great historical movements which are not to be criticised or corrected, but which impose upon the student the convictions which he is to adopt.

2. It is plain from a correct statement of the facts that the action of Germany in demonetizing silver was by no means arbitrary. It had the fullest motives and occasion in the state of that nation, and its interest and convenience.[2]

3. The action of the Scandinavian nations was not arbitrary or destitute of motive. The movement towards gold was now so far advanced that the small nations were forced to join it in self-defence. The last to join it would be loaded with the discarded silver, and would have to endure a large part of the total loss upon it. This is only an illustration of the rapid impulse with which such movements finally complete themselves, when the forces have acquired momentum.

4. The action of the United States in 1873 was guided by

[1] Mr. Horton (Report, p. 240). Mr. Horton speaks (p. 745) of the "partisans of gold and persecutors of silver."

[2] The argument of Gen. Walker before the Conference was based upon the assertion that Germany's action was arbitrary. See Report, p. 74.

previous legislation, custom, fact, convenience, and the interests of the country, as they then appeared, and, so far as any evidence has ever been brought forward, by nothing else.

B. We come now to the latest incident in this historical development—a case of action which was indeed arbitrary and destitute of motive. The United States were in currency trouble of their own, serious enough and difficult enough, in itself considered, but they enjoyed, from the suspension of specie payments, one incidental advantage. They had no part or lot in the silver difficulty.[1] They had no stock of silver on which to suffer loss. Their laws were in proper shape to secure resumption on the best system of coinage yet devised. They had time before them. They could wait for developments and take advantage of any state of affairs which might arise, without taking any speculative risks at all. Mr. Horton thinks the United States had a great interest because the demonetization of silver made resumption harder. Resumption on silver would have been easier than resumption on gold, just as resumption would have been easier if the gold dollar had been reduced ten per cent in weight, and not otherwise. In this state of things, then, the United States wilfully plunged into the silver difficulty, and, moreover, came forward to tell those who were in silver difficulty how to get out, and volunteered to lead the way. All the other nations represented at the Conference had an interest in the silver problem, but all refused to act, with the possible exception of Italy. The United States had no interest, but nevertheless took action. As a consequence, this nation now has thirty million dollars of capital invested in silver, which is lying idle and cannot be disposed of without loss. This sum and a large amount in trade dollars have been retained at home as a new element of disorder in our currency, instead of following their natural course to the East. If the advocates of free coinage for silver had had their way, we should also have received thirty or forty millions in silver instead of the same amount in gold received this Fall. Mr. Horton is of opinion that this was a noble ac-

---

[1] I suppose it is necessary to say that the interest of American silver producers was no interest of the United States. The iron producers were in worse trouble than the silver producers, but no one proposed that the nation should expend capital to "bull" iron.

tion, on the part of the United States on behalf of mankind in general, which has rarely been paralleled. It was, in fact, a piece of national Quixotism which has no parallel in history. The same writer quotes this action as an exception or offset to the uniform tendency of the historical events above cited, but its arbitrary and unfounded character rob it of any force for such a deduction.

IV. It is impossible that I should, within the limits of the present article, review and criticise the points raised at the Conference. Two or three of the chief of them here demand brief attention.

1. The American delegates began by slandering the legislalation of their country, and it was left for a foreigner to show (1) that the historical facts about the legislation of 1873 were incorrectly stated by the American delegates, and (2) that the United States are a constitutional country, not ruled by plebiscites, and that we cannot plead ignorance on the part of "the people" against legislation constitutionally adopted. Gen. Walker endeavored to sustain the allegations of his colleague by saying that he, although a professor of political economy, engaged, at the time, in lecturing on money, did not know what was going on. It does not appear that this argument elicited any reply. Perhaps it was thought that its force all lay in the recoil, and some wonder may have been excited whether all American economists would have been obliged to say the same. The fact is that the Act of 1873 so simply enacted the existing law and facts that no one attributed any importance to it.

2. The chief reasons adduced for the action proposed by the United States were vague and undefined terrors of consequences from the historical movement we have described. It was alleged that half the money in the world has been cancelled. This assertion has no foundation in fact. The amount demonetized is just exactly what has been demonetized, viz., the amount of silver held by Germany and the Scandinavian States, and to this there have been important offsets. In the first place, there has been the production of gold since 1873, which, according to Soetbeer's calculations,[1] must have averaged one hundred and

---

[1] *Edelmetall-Production (Petermann's Mittheilungen, Erg. Heft No. 57, p. 112).*

twenty million dollars per annum. In the second place, all the silver five-franc pieces in existence have been added to the stock of "money." Before the fall in silver they were worth more than gold and were merchandise. Since they fell to an equality with gold (below it in value; held equal by limitation [1]), they have been available as money. It would be very difficult to show that, comparing 1879 with 1873, there has been any contraction whatever of the metallic money of Europe and the United States. The expansions and contractions of paper money in Europe and North and South America, within twenty years, have had far greater influence on credit and prices the world over than the changes connected with silver.

3. The fear was also expressed that the adoption of gold would destroy the par of exchange with silver countries, and it was urged that the bimetallic system would furnish a "normal" par. What is the "par" of exchange? Exchange is a ratio between two quantities. How can the ratio between two quantities be "destroyed" so long as the quantities exist? The par of exchange is an entirely imaginary mean-line between fluctuations which are constant, and it has no importance except for the academic explanation of phenomena. We can make a "normal" par any minute; $\$4.44 = £1$ is as good a par as any. The sovereign and the dollar may then each of them be gold, silver, or anything else; their values will have a ratio to each other, and may be stated in percentages of $4.44.

V. I proposed, however, to examine the bimetallic notion in its essence, and to proceed with that task it is necessary to consider the relation of legislation to value.[2] For the exposition of the bimetallic fallacy, as well as a number of others which are now widely held and even taught, it is necessary to show that legislation cannot affect value at all. If it could, the text-books of political economy are very faulty in their analysis of value, since no one of them specifies legislation amongst the forces by which value is controlled.

---

[1] The Bank of France in September charged one tenth of one per cent premium on gold over silver.—*Economist*, Sept. 6, p. 1026.

[2] "Let me dwell upon the fundamental error which suggests the measure which has been proposed. That error is the belief that it appertains to governments to call value into existence." (Mr. Pirmez. Report, p. 121.)

1. The value of a thing is controlled by supply and demand and by nothing else. Supply and demand are natural forces and act under natural laws. By this we mean that supply and demand spring into action from the presence, in certain relations to each other, of certain natural facts. The natural facts, in this case, are (1) a society of men having certain needs, and (2) material goods fit to satisfy those needs. The needs of the men for the goods do not exist because the men so choose, but because they are men. The goods are not supply for the needs because the men so decide, but by virtue of natural qualities. Supply and demand are therefore complementary parts of a force which is natural in the same sense that any physical force is natural. This force must arise when its natural conditions exist; it cannot arise unless they exist; when it arises it acts under natural law—that is, produces a regular succession of phenomena in a determined sequence—and the statement of the law in human language must be made by describing the conditions of equilibrium between the complementary parts, since it is by their equilibrium that the supply performs its function, and the needs receive satisfaction, and the economic force is merged in the vital force of man. The action of man on natural forces is restricted to dividing, combining, and diverting them. He can neither create nor destroy them. The forces may be divided, but the sum of the effects must always be perfectly proportioned to the force, neither less nor more. If any portion of the force is missing in the effect, our task is not complete until we have followed it, ascertained its incidence and effect, and united it to the rest.

2. Gold has its own conditions of supply and demand, and silver has its own conditions of supply and demand, and they are both independent of each other. Those conditions are facts in regard to the actual existence of the metals within the reach of man on the one side, and the increasing, decreasing, or changing needs of the human race, as it lives its life on earth, upon the other. Legislation can affect these conditions in no respect whatever. It cannot increase or decrease the amount of the metals within the reach of man, or his willingness to labor to produce them according to the profit of such production. It cannot make men want what they do not want, or cease to want

what they do want. Economic phenomena are due to economic forces, and one of the first lessons the student has to learn is not to rest from his analysis until he has reduced economic phenomena to economic forces and laws.

One might as well tell a physiologist that his science is false because no man ever existed whose organs were all perfectly normal in their functions, as to contradict an economist because no man ever acted from purely economic motives. Indeed the absurdity is far greater in the latter case, since the economist deals with societies, not individuals; so that not only is the inference unfounded, but the fact alleged is untrue of societies. One might as well object against a physiologist, when he states physiological laws, that moral forces (or, rather, more or less immoral forces, for that is what we mean) affect the bodily functions, as to interpose the objection against economic laws that immoral forces affect economic phenomena. The fact in both cases is undeniable; the inference—that these external interferences alter natural forces and laws, and therefore ought to be taken into account in the statement of scientific principles—is equally unfounded in both. One might as well tell a physiologist that a knife thrust into an organ alters physiological forces and laws, as to tell an economist that legislation controls the laws of value. It is because the physiological laws are not altered that the victim dies. The hygiene, pathology, and therapeutics of society are mixed with its physiology in our text-books, but the scientific distinctions must be maintained intact if we would reason correctly. Value belongs to the physiology of society, legislation almost always to its pathology. Legislation creates the conditions of disease, leads to distorted organs, disordered functions, deceptive phenomena (§ 4 below), and taxes the sagacity and clear-headedness of the student to find again the normal forces in their distorted action; but we have to guard ourselves well against the delusion that it changes forces or laws. To adopt that delusion is to lose perception of the difference between social health and social disease. We are struggling here for the introduction into political economy of universal canons of science which are recognized in all other departments which enjoy authority and are making real progress.

3. One chief cause of the notion amongst us that legislation

can regulate the value of money is, no doubt, the provision in the Constitution of the United States that Congress shall have power so to do. Why was it not also provided, in connection with the cognate power "to fix the standard of weights and measures," that Congress might regulate the length and weight of things? Here is a table. It is so long. How long? Just the quantity of extension in one dimension which it has as a physical fact. If you were here, you would see it. As you are not, I have recourse to ratios to other extensions which you do know. It has the same length as the distance from a man's nose to the end of his middle finger. The Congress of the United States, however, has provided an arbitrary standard of length, now grown familiar by use, and if I write that this table is a yard long, it will be a far more convenient and accurate designation, because it will refer to a more accurate length, equally familiar. If Congress had adopted a standard yard as long as what we now call a foot, that would have become familiar, I should then have written three yards instead of one, and the knowledge conveyed would have been the same. Now how large a Congressional majority would it take to make this table one thousandth of an inch longer or shorter than it actually is? The parallel with the case of money is complete. The Constitution of the United States could not confer powers which nature has never given to mankind. Congress cannot regulate the value of money until it can make a man give for a gold dollar one grain of wheat more than supply and demand force him to give, or yield a gold dollar for one grain less than supply and demand will give him for it. To regulate the value of money is to fix prices, and Congress has never tried that since it has existed. Congress can determine how heavy a piece of metal of a certain fineness shall be the standard of value, just as it determines how long a bar shall be the standard of length; but it cannot regulate the value of a coin any more than it can regulate a physical object to make it longer or shorter than it is.

4. The cases of apparent interference with supply and demand by individuals, combinations, and governments are all cases of monopoly, which is only a special case of supply and demand. An artificial monopoly is possible whenever the supply is capable of comprehension and limitation, and the ma-

nipulation of a monopoly consists in so limiting the supply and adjusting it to the demand as to make the market take some amount at some price. If the monopolist wants to sell more, he must yield on his price. If he wants a higher price, he must be content to sell less. It would be a great mistake, however, to say that a monopolist controls value. It is just because he does not control value that he makes anything. There is still a true point of equilibrium which supply and demand would reach, if free, and it is out of the margin between that point and the point at which the monopolist fixes the market price that his gains, as monopolist, come. There is no other scientific explanation of those gains. A "corner" is a modified case of monopoly, in which the first action is exerted upon the demand. All offered is bought at a price above what any other buyer will pay. This operation, however, is only preliminary to the formation of a monopoly, and a monopoly sale. It would be senseless unless there was a demand foreseen, which would, for some reason, be so strong as to ensure the monopolists a sale at a price above what they pay. What the monopolist does, then, in either case, is to fix the ratio at which the exchange actually takes place at a different ratio from that which value would establish. He thereby transfers other men's goods to himself without giving any equivalent, and it is precisely because value gives us a second point of comparison that we are able to say that the action of the monopolist is unjust and oppressive, and that monopolies are justly odious.

5. The apparent cases of legislative interference with value are cases in point. Subsidiary coins are a case of monopoly, and the problem of their management is to limit the supply to the demand of the community for said coins at their nominal value. Paper money is a case of monopoly. The problem of its value, which has troubled so many writers, is to hold the supply at or below the demand of the community for money to do its business with at par with coin. If the supply of paper dollars is made to exceed the number of gold dollars which the country would need, they will no longer hold a value equal to the value of a gold dollar each. The tariff is a case of monopoly. The protected producers can get the market price plus the tariff, only by selling less than the community would take

at the market price. If they increase the supply, they may run down the price in the home market below the price in the world's market. Hence paper money transfers property from its just possessors to the issuers of the paper, without equivalent, and tariffs transfer property from the unprotected owners to the protected producers without an equivalent. The extent to which this takes place depends on the manipulation of the monopoly; the effect of legislation is limited to the creation of the opportunity for a monopoly.

6. Legal-tender laws, when they are what they ought to be, simply enactments of what is the universal custom and understanding, are rarely if ever called into action at all. It seems to be forgotten that this is their original and only proper character, and whenever such laws are proposed or referred to, laws are always meant which involve some coercion, or distortiom of the terms of a contract. Legal-tender laws of this character do not alter truth, justice, or value. They only transfer property. A legal-tender law does not make 90 paid = 100 due a true equation. The only true equation is 90 paid + 10 retained = 100 due. Legal-tender laws alter the line between mine and thine so that something which was on one side is now on the other, but they do not affect the validity of the venerable distinction. The legal-tender law simply provides that the courts which administer justice under the Constitution and laws of the country in question shall not listen, in certain cases, to the plea of the citizen who complains of injustice; in other words, it withdraws the protection of the courts of justice, in certain cases, from citizens who complain of injustice. Some decisions even seem to go so far as to interpret the law so that A may demand B's property and discharge B's claim with an arbitrary allowance to which B never consented. In all cases it is because the forces of nature act in perfect fidelity to their laws that we can see and define the injustice of this legislation. It is because the legislation has not affected the law of value that we can have another state of things in mind as right and just, and can often measure the degree to which legislation has transferred the products of one man's labor and economy to another man's use and enjoyment. It would be difficult indeed to prove that the value of a man's property or his right to it

was affected by stealing it from him. Value is one form of truth, and truth is not affected by majorities. The notion that legislation affects value must therefore be positively condemned as the root-error of a dozen mischievous fallacies. Legislation transfers property, and that is all it ever does.

7. It is necessary to notice also the law which governs all combinations. If a single individual undertakes, for instance, to establish a corner, he may be reasonably sure of his own will, intention, and plan, and may carry it out if he does not lose his head and prove inconsistent with himself—which indeed sometimes occurs. If he finds it necessary to associate another with himself, there arises the need of selecting a congenial comrade and of securing consent, co-operation, loyalty, and good faith between two separate wills. The difficulty of such combination is not double that of an individual operation; it may be twentyfold greater. If three, five, ten, twenty persons must be combined, the difficulty advances in a tremendous ratio until it becomes a practical impossibility. Hence the manipulation of a corner or a monopoly does not gain force or become easier as the task is widened and the number of participants is increased, but the force decreases in an enormous ratio to the extension of the party, and the practical chances of success diminish in an equally rapid ratio to the number of participants.

VI. Having elucidated these points, which, by the way, show the need, in economic discussions, of firm grasp of elementary notions and principles, we may, in a brief space, bring them to bear on the thesis with which we started.

1. Inasmuch as gold and silver have independent conditions of supply and demand in natural facts, their relative value may remain the same through a long period, or one or the other may grow dearer, and the fluctuations may be rare or frequent, wide or narrow, sudden or gradual, in all possible combinations and sequences. It has been proposed to form an international union, to establish a fixed ratio for the mints of all members of the union, and to make either metal legal tender. By this plan it is proposed to change from one metal to the other as fluctuations take place, and it is expected that the fluctuations will be limited in their range, but it is not expected that a concurrent circulation will be produced, or that the whole

stock of both metals will be brought to act on credit and prices. Reserving for the present the question of the practicability of the coinage union, it may be admitted that, under some circumstances, the fluctuations would be limited, but they would be more frequent and sudden, and the system would be at the sport of chance, as the Latin Union was. These, however, are minor difficulties. The legal-tender law, by which all this is to be accomplished, would simply, as above shown, transfer property. The gain, if any, would be a gain to some at the expense of others. In plain language, the project is one for uniting the debtor classes of all civilized nations in a "corner" on the falling metal. Such a project has no parallel save in some of the wildest plans of the International Society. The profits of the corner would come out of the creditor class and the holders of the rising metal. It would be establishing on a world-wide scale, and by force of law, an injustice by which some men would throw the risks and loss of their business on other men, who already have the risks and losses of their own business to carry. For instance, some Liverpool merchants interested in the South American and East Indian trade have suffered loss by the fall in silver. They are eager for the "double standard" to save them from their losses, and no doubt it would do so, but only by throwing those losses on the whole creditor class of England. Now, the creditor class of England is scattered, unorganized, and unknown, but it is safe to say that it has its own troubles from business and investments, and is suffering from loss of dividends, failure of banks, fall in prices, fall in rents, fire, shipwreck, and all the other chances and accidents of life. The advocates of the "alternate standard" have contented themselves with dilating upon the effect of their scheme in narrowing the fluctuations of the market rate of the metals, without reflecting that no such effect could be attained without an expenditure of force, at somebody's expense, elsewhere.

2. But the coinage union is a practical impossibility. France, a country with a free mint for both metals, standing between Germany, a silver country, and England, a gold country, was able to work a compensatory action between them. There is an obvious fallacy, however, in reasoning that the same action would go on, on a larger scale and with greater efficiency, if the differ-

entiation upon which the interaction depended were obliterated in a coinage union having a uniform system.

There is a further fallacy, and a far more serious one from a scientific point of view, in supposing that the coinage union, if extended, would gain proportionate increments of force to restrain fluctuations until they were reduced to a minimum or to nothing. The law above stated here comes into operation, by virtue of which a combination becomes not stronger, but weaker, as it is extended, and the attempt of all nations to form a corner upon the falling metal would dissipate itself like a corner which united all the buyers—that is, it would become simply identical with demand as we ordinarily use the term. Instead, therefore, of marching towards a realization of bimetallism or a concurrent circulation, the coinage union would work towards the simple free play of natural forces, in which each metal would obey its own conditions of supply and demand. Nor is this all. The coinage union is either unnecessary, or else it is needed in order to impose a set line of action and to enforce co-operation where voluntary co-operation would not be given. How can any one believe that sovereign nations will enter into any such combination, or that, if they did enter into it, they would stay in and obey mandates which conflicted with their interest and will? We are not left to speculation as to the probability that they would so act. We have two facts to which to refer: (1) When the fall in silver took place, the Latin Union would have been disrupted by the secession of Belgium and Switzerland if the coinage of silver had not been suspended. (2) The commissioners of the Latin Union, at their last meeting, agreed that Italy should withdraw her small notes to make room for the return of her small coin with which the other states, especially France, were burdened. I do not understand that Italy has refused to do this, but the remonstrances which were made in the Italian Parliament against this dictation as to what Italy should do with her own currency were just what must be expected in such a case, and they show that an international coinage union would prove a rope of sand so soon as the attempt was made to make it efficient at all. An international coinage union, therefore, to accomplish a definite and set purpose in turning back a movement which all recognize, whether they deplore it or not, is an absolutely impracticable scheme.

3. I have never seen any argument for the feasibility of bimetallism, or a concurrent circulation, in which the whole of both metals would act on prices and credit, except the facile inference that the coinage union as it grew larger would or might restrain fluctuations more and more, to a minimum or to nothing. As I have broken down every assumption here involved, the inference falls to the ground. It appears that this reasoning follows neither a true relation of facts nor any logical sequence. The coinage union as it grew larger and larger would grow less and less effective, and when it was complete it would have no effect at all. The notion of a concurrent circulation is therefore entirely baseless—snatched from the air. So long as the natural conditions of supply and demand of gold and silver remained the same, whether for a longer or shorter period, so long the forces would remain the same, and the effects would remain the same. So soon, whether sooner or later, as the conditions varied, the forces would vary, and the proportionate effects would vary. To secure a concurrent circulation, then, at a fixed ratio, it is necessary to suppress the effects, which can only be done by suppressing the forces, so that a concurrent circulation could never be realized until we could extinguish economic forces by human agency. But we can no more extinguish a force than we can create one, so that this scheme is in economics what perpetual motion is in mechanics. Every analysis that is attempted of the idea will only issue in new proof that it is an absurdity which cannot be thought, and it is no longer strange that its advocates have never been able to state their notion in intelligible language. It must remain vague, shadowy, and popular, stated at best in symbols, metaphors, and analogies, to exist at all.[1]

VII. If the amount of space which would be required were not out of all proportion to the results for our purpose, I should

---

[1] "As for the desire which has been expressed that the hope be left open that some day a fixed relation may be established between gold and silver and an international value given to them, the English delegate (Mr. Goschen) declared that, in his view, it was impossible to realize this, impossible to maintain it in theory, and that it was contrary to the principles of science." (Report, p. 166.)

like to analyze some of the analogies which have been employed in this discussion. Some of them deserve to be put into the text-books on logic as classical examples of the mischief of reasoning by analogy. An analogy proves nothing whatever. It only serves to state a theorem in a form to be more easily apprehended. The theorem, then, needs to be proven by its appropriate demonstration. After showing the mischievous character of the notions imported into this discussion by the analogies of tubs of water joined by a tube, and horses driven in span, I should not have advanced the discussion in which I am engaged. The bimetallist says: A concurrent circulation seems to me like driving two horses in span. I answer: To me it seems like yoking the sun and moon together to facilitate the reckoning of time by men by making the lunar month a simple fraction of the solar year. Nothing is accomplished by these statements towards testing the truth of either opinion. I therefore pass by all the analogies which have been offered by the bimetallists with the simple remark that they are all untrue and misleading.

The advocates of the goloid dollar, who think they can give greater fixity to the ratio of the metals by mixing them in the same coin, advocate a more grotesque absurdity, but not a greater one, than the other advocates of a "concurrent circulation."

VIII. We must infer, then, that gold and silver will both be used as components in the world's money, by the adoption by some nations of one and by other nations of the other, as their convenience and interest dictate. The United States, by its legislation so far, has put itself on the way to become one of the silver countries. It is not a dogmatic judgment; it is inference from observation of the course adopted by nations, that gold is more convenient for the purpose of the leading commercial nations, and silver for those which are yet behind.[1] The United States is one of those whose interests require the use of gold, and the way back over the path we are now treading will have to be won by trouble, loss, and inconvenience. Our children, instead of admiring our Quixotic devotion to mankind

[1] Feer-Herzog. Report, p. 60.

in general, will ask us how we could ever commit the folly of plunging into a difficulty which everybody else was trying to escape, and from which our children will have to extricate themselves at heavy expense. I am far from denying that the change from silver to gold is attended by loss and inconvenience, but I do not know of any step of social or economic advance which has ever been made without temporary loss and inconvenience both to capital and labor, and the United States were not exposed to any of this loss at all. Mr. Seyd has just published a book, "The Decline of Prosperity, and its Insidious Cause," in which, as the title indicates, he takes a very lugubrious view of things, and ascribes the mischief to the demonetization of silver. This fear that prosperity was declining has come up every fifteen or twenty years for a century or two, especially in England, and yet prosperity and civilization advance. In 1872 coal and meat were dear, and the newspapers were filled with essays about the sufferings of the people on fixed incomes. Then the woes of the agricultural laborers came up, and the farmers were represented as selfish men, gorged with wealth and prosperity. Now meat is too cheap, the turn has come to the landowners, and the farmers are the objects of public concern. Such changes are the inevitable effects of the continual changes in the conditions of industry and the relations of commerce. It is from and by means of such changes that the prosperity of mankind advances. Every great improvement involves changes and readjustments. They are not welcome, but they are unavoidable. It is not at all improbable that the number and variety of the great improvements of the last twenty years, following so rapidly on each other, crossing and combining with each other, necessitating quick and complicated adjustments, may go for a great deal in the present reaction. It is very probable that the next twenty-five years are to see massive migrations of population, and great transfers of capital, from the old to the new countries, which will not be made until suffering has enforced them. It is probable that the value and rent of land will decline in the old countries and rise in the new. It is possible that social, economic, and political changes· are to be accomplished such as we cannot yet guess at. It is certain to my mind, however, that those years are to be years of unprecedented prosperity.

The fall in silver has its share in the temporary disorder, loss, and suffering; but the use of the single gold standard will be one of the strongest supports of the new prosperity. If this were not so, it would be idle to lament over a movement which comes along in the natural evolution of things. To try to stem that movement and turn it back to the old system of repeated empirical struggles for a bimetallic circulation, it would be necessary for us to be sure of three things: (1) that we understand present phenomena thoroughly,[1] (2) that we can foresee the results of the movement towards gold, if it goes on, and (3) that we are sure of the working of the gigantic experiment involved in the attempt to secure bimetallism, or the alternate standard, by a coinage union. These conditions are absolutely unfulfilled. On the contrary, it seems that international banking is just at the point where its further development, and the transfer of capital from old to new countries, above alluded to, require an international standard of value amongst the great commercial nations such as gold alone can supply. The development of international banking, in its turn, will economize the use of gold, and thus again defeat the fears of those who think there is not gold enough. The movement, therefore, bears all the marks of a true organic development, in which all the parts contribute to and support each other in advancement to a higher stage. It also seems to me that the fall in silver is precisely adapted to favor those extensions of commerce and civilization which lie in the near future. South America is still in the lowest stage of economic development, and will find silver its best money for a long time to come. Asia is scarcely yet upon a monetary system, except where Europeans have penetrated, and can use nothing but silver to advantage for an indefinite future. Africa is an almost untouched continent, which, within fifty years, will probably come into new

---

[1] The authorities are by no means agreed as to the causes of the fall of silver. This question came up at Paris, and Mr. Feer-Herzog maintained that the key to the phenomenon lay in the state of the East Indian exchanges. (Report, p. 58.) This is the view which I took before the U. S. Silver Committee in 1876, but I have never seen any other confirmation of it.

relations to the civilized world. Silver is the only suitable medium for this extension of commerce. As far, then, as we can foresee, the cheapening of the tool of exchange by which these extensions of trade and civilization must be carried on will only facilitate them; and if bimetallism were not an absurdity, and the alternate standard either an injustice or a delusion, and if either of them were practicable, the adoption of either would now be the grandest mistake the civilized world could commit. I attribute no weight to these prognostications of mine. It is contrary to my opinion of sound procedure in such matters to make them at all. I should consider it the most vicious procedure to make such prognostications the basis of argument that any nation or that all civilized nations "ought" to use the single gold standard. The economic development of human society must go on its way and work out its results, and the human race must make the best of them. The race, however, does not make mistakes, and so long as, in all its parts, it obeys the dictates of its interests, it will push on a true evolution which cannot but serve to enhance the prosperity of the race as a whole. It is only when nations allow their action to be dictated by speculations about the future of civilization and humanity that they may wreck the natural development. It is because these terrors about the future, and prophecies of disaster, have been introduced to play so great a *rôle* on the other side of this question that I venture to set against them the best speculations I can make as to the probable course of affairs.

POSTSCRIPT.—After the above was in type my attention was called, by an editorial in the New York *Tribune*, to a recantation by Mr. Gibbs of the opinions maintained by him at the Conference at Paris. The plan of my article was to make an independent discussion, and not to examine the literature of bimetallism beyond the Report of the Monetary Commission. When, however, a journal which has sustained a uniformly sound and strong position on monetary questions referred to Mr. Gibbs' pamphlet in the terms used by the *Tribune*, it seemed that here perhaps a bimetallist might at last be found who had some clear ideas, and could state them so as to bear examination. I therefore hastened to secure a copy of Mr. Gibbs' pamphlet,[1] and also a copy of his letter to Cernuschi announcing his conversion, and Cernuschi's reply to the same.[2] My hopes of finding something in these pamphlets solid enough to bear examination for purposes of discussion are all disappointed.

Mr. Gibbs has simply gone over to the bimetallic fallacy, and accepted it in its grossest and crudest form. He has produced no new arguments for it and refuted no objections against it. Incidentally he has shown that the ex-Governor of the Bank of England holds, in regard to money, all the fallacies which constitute the premises of our soft-money men; and if he does not agree with them in their conclusions, it is only because he is less logical and consistent. This, however, might be said of all bimetallists. The *Tribune's* estimate of this pamphlet adds the greatest possible weight to the motive for my article as stated in the first paragraph thereof. I am therefore led to counteract that estimate by amplifying one or two points which I had passed over briefly, and by inserting one or two which I had judged better to omit, in order to show the real significance and value of what Mr. Gibbs has contributed to this controversy.

1. Mr. Gibbs' conversion to bimetallism is due to observation of the losses incurred in Indian finances and Indian trade. He assumes that these losses are due to the fall in silver, and he attributes the fall in silver to demonetization. Hence he argues: Remonetize; that will restore silver; that will stop the losses. It is a pity that the matter is not so simple. I consider it an error to attribute the losses in the India trade to the fall in silver. The fall in silver is not a cause, but a consequence. The financial relations between England and India after 1870 took such shape that the "tribute," as it is called, had to be paid by an excess of exports over imports of India. This could only be accomplished by a fall in prices in India. Nevertheless Europe desired to continue to sell silver to India, while the relation just mentioned would have led

---

[1] "Silver and Gold," by Henry H. Gibbs, London, 1879.
[2] "Bimetallism in England and Abroad," by Henri Cernuschi, London, 1879.

India to desist from buying it. Instead of a *fall* in prices (silver remaining stable) there therefore has occurred the exactly equivalent phenomenon of a fall in silver *without any rise* in prices. In countries which have a depreciated paper currency prices rise as the medium falls, and so the foreign trade quickly adjusts itself. If prices had risen in India there would have been no trouble; but the forces which would have forced a fall in prices if silver had held firm have prevented a rise in prices while forcing a fall in the medium. A crisis in the Indian exchanges was therefore inevitable in some form or other. Instead of taking place through prices, it has taken place through the medium—silver—and the fall in silver, is a consequence and not a cause. This relation of facts accounts for the fall in silver, and nothing else does. The silver thrown on the market by demonetization and by a somewhat increased production (which has been greatly exaggerated) by no means account for the fall. The increased supply fell on a weak market, and had accessory influence, but it does not suffice to account for the principal effect. It follows that it is a great error for those who suffer from losses in the India trade to ascribe their troubles to the fall in silver, and that their troubles cannot be cured by any currency devices. While India has so much interest to pay in England on borrowed capital, to which she has not yet grown up, and while she has to pay in England for an expensive government, to which also she has not yet grown up, she will be a worse country to sell in and a better one to buy in than formerly. However, if English merchants and bankers interested in the India trade could sell their silver to somebody for the old price, it is obvious that they could save themselves from the effect of these changed circumstances in the relations of the two countries.

2. This last observation leads me to amplify what I have said under VI., 1. I have shown there that the alternate standard would only transfer risks and losses from those to whom they belong to somebody else. *A fortiori* bimetallism, if it were practicable, would throw all risks and losses, all the time, on the creditor classes. Gibbs and Cernuschi seem to be entirely blind to this character in their propositions, and they do not see that whatever they gain for some must either be won out of others

or *out of nothing*, as I have shown in my main argument. To show this more fully, let us observe the difference for different classes between the significance of a fall in gold and the significance of a fall in silver. The effect of a fall in gold (rise in prices) would fall on annuitants, pensioners, owners of bonds, etc., beneficiaries of trusts and life assurances, salaried and professional men, wage-receivers, and, generally, on all who have either temporarily or permanently fixed incomes. These are the persons whom I designate as the creditor classes. A fall in silver, as things stood in 1873, affected producers, exchangers, and bankers in certain great lines of business. A fall in gold would therefore affect a large number of small, weak, and scattered recipients of money incomes, belonging to different classes and having no co-operation or even acquaintance with each other. A fall in silver affects great "interests," each of which is marked by very strong cohesion of its parts within itself, and all of which are capable of sudden and easy combination. The former have little power or chance to defend themselves; the latter are powerful and influential in speech, writing, and legislation. The former never attract public attention; the latter fill the public eye and are thought of whenever money, capital, trade, or industry are thought of. The losses of the latter make up appalling figures in the statistics of bankruptcy. The losses of the former figure in no statistics, since they consist in privation, misery, disease, and earlier death for those affected directly and for their dependants. The losses to producers, exchangers, and bankers are what govern the opinions of Mr. Seyd, and now, too, have converted Mr. Gibbs. It is indeed cause for great regret that such losses should occur, and if there were any means of averting the loss altogether, the matter would bear a very different aspect. But there is no such means. There is nothing possible but an alternative, either to leave the losses where they fall by the circumstances of the case, or to throw them on somebody else; and nothing is proposed in these monetary schemes save to throw the losses on those who would have suffered if the fall had been in gold instead of in silver. Now when gold has fallen (prices have risen), notably in 1870-1873, the classes who were affected had to make the best of it without aid from those interested in silver, and so the proposition that

England shall now adopt bimetallism, when stripped of all disguises, is simply another case of the old abuse whereby a few strong, well-organized interests, acting through currency legislation, play at "heads I win, tails you lose" with the large, scattered, unorganized mass of the nation. English statesmen may possibly upset the monetary basis on which all relations of property and credit in England rest, in order to alleviate a temporary strain on some branches of foreign trade, and on the finances of India; but those who have to rely on American newspapers for their information and impressions of what is likely to be done in this matter in Europe will do well to nourish an active incredulousness. Those Americans who have to rely on the Hon. W. D. Kelly's reports of interviews between himself and Bismarck for judgments as to the probable course of Germany will do well to allow for other elements in the report than the probable power of Mr. Kelly to inspire the Prince with expansive and familiar confidence. Mr. Kelly is a man of enthusiastic imagination, and it appears probable that he and Mr. George Walker are just the kind of men to excite the well-known propensity of the German Chancellor to befool people by an ostentatious and effusive frankness while laughing at them in his sleeve. A great deal has been said about the zeal, dogmatism, and fanaticism of the advocates of the single universal gold standard. I do not know who these persons are, nor what they have done. The only persons who, in regard to this monetary question, have organized a sect, adopted a creed, undertaken a propaganda, and sent out missionaries, so far as I know, are the bimetallists. It is charitable to believe that they do not see the political and social significance of their propositions, but that statesmen will not see this long before action is adopted is very improbable.

Now Mr. Gibbs has just found out that the trade between India and England is barter. He is astonished and alarmed at this. He thinks this kind of trade uncivilized and attended by loss to England. He attributes the evil to English gold monometallism, and thinks that the evil effects have been counteracted until recent years by the French law. If it be true, however, as Mr. Gibbs and the other bimetallists argue, that France has done this service by her law, now to gold-using Englishmen and now to silver-using Germans, then France, through her creditor class, has borne burdens and losses which belonged to other people. Such being the case, we could see why Englishmen and Germans should want the French law to continue, but we should also see why Frenchmen, so soon as they understood it, would certainly want it to stop; and, if universal bimetallism could be or should be established, the next question would be, What class, under the new system, is to take the place formerly filled by the French creditor class and bear the burdens formerly borne by them?

Such is the inference from Mr. Gibbs' premisses, but the premisses are false. Trade with India is barter, but so is all trade, and foreign trade most plainly. The trade for silver has involved inconveniences which will exist until all the world uses a single and universal standard of value. This inconvenience has been paid for, as all other hindrances and difficulties of trade are paid for, in prices. The French mint law has had nothing to do with it. Finally, the French creditors have lost whenever the ratio of the metals has varied so as to change the metal of the French coinage. This loss, however, has been borne once for all; it has not continued after prices have been readjusted; and has not therefore been constant under the operation of the double standard.

Cernuschi, in his reply to Gibbs, gives far more gross expression to the same fallacy about the operation of the French law to prevent losses; for he attaches it not to English traders, but to all metal producers. "At the time of the French 15½, the position of the producers of gold and silver was this: all their produce had by law an unfailing and insatiable customer —the *mint*. No price to haggle about, no competition possible." A customer by law! The mint a customer!? In some large establishments, as a check on salesmen, one person is stationed at a counter to weigh, measure, and count all goods for which the salesmen have made bargains with the customers. It would be as sensible to call this person the "unfailing and insatiable customer" for all the goods sold in the establishment as to call the mint a customer for gold and silver. This gross error, however, is the cloak which covers the fallacy and the injustice of bimetallism. The law does provide a customer, but it is not the mint. It is the creditor class as above defined. There is "no price to haggle about and no competition to fear" because the law has delivered the victim over helpless, all the more helpless because he is ignorant, the law having concealed the transaction under mysteries of coinage and money. This, however, is the most direct condemnation of the law itself, as well in an economic as a social or political point of view. It is a fallacy to think the mint law has secured the producers of the metals against loss and haggling and competition—that is, against all the inevitable annoyances of industry without hurting anybody else ; and it is an injustice to take the annoyances from one industry only to spread them over others. I do not like to say anything which may appear arrogant and unbecoming, but I feel justified in protesting, in the name of all that scholars and scientific men respect, that a man who calls the mint an " unfailing and insatiable customer" does not deserve respectful treatment in the arena of scientific discussion.

Mr. Gibbs sees that bimetallism involves depreciation, but he thinks the evils of it are in this case more nominal than real. The only distinction which men generally make between nominal evils and real evils is that my evils are real and yours are nominal; but that is not a valid distinction which science or justice can recognize. Mr. Gibbs seems to think the evils of depreciation nominal because they would be widely scattered and much concealed, as I have shown above. All evils, however, are real to those who suffer them. If they come from nature, like blight, drought, storms, inundations, and other calamities, they must be borne as philosophically as possible. If they are inflicted by legislation, or are transferred by legislation, nothing can justify or belittle them. Mr. Gibbs wants silver remonetized, not at its present market value, but at the point where it will be when the bimetallic system shall have operated on it. He has not comprehended the full problem which he has to solve. It is this: (1) If in England, for instance, silver is rated at its present market value, all the silver now in England loses 20 per cent of its present value. (2) If silver is rated at the point to which the bimetallic system will bring it up, no one but Cernuschi knows where that will be. If a guess is made, and silver is rated above the market, no debtor will want it, and so the bimetallic system will never begin. (3) If silver is rated at the market to begin with, and if the mint ratio is advanced as the market ratio advances (assuming that bimetallism would work), then continual recoinage, with heavy expense and endless confusion, will result. I hope that it is plain, then, that the bimetallists of every grade and description are either trying to transfer losses from one group of men to another, or else trying to make something out of nothing.

3. It also seems desirable to notice another error of bimetallism which I had passed over; that is the notion that demand due to a fall in price raises price. This doctrine is essential to the bimetallic theory, and it has been carelessly conceded by some who are not bimetallists. I passed over it in the body of my article because it is the fallacy of that extreme form of bimetallism in which it is believed that the coinage union will lock the two metals so tight together that they will never separate from the legal ratio any more, because there will be no one to whom to sell the rising metal. Every bimetallist would be driven to this doctrine if he followed out his notions consistently; but the bimetallists repudiate it generally when it is ascribed to them. Mr. Gibbs, however, explicitly accepts this notion, and assumes that the bimetallic union would lock the two metals permanently together as such an undoubted fact that it is his chief reliance for refuting objections. Demand due to a fall in price tends to sustain price at the lower level, but not to raise price, since such demand ceases when the price rises. If we have a bimetallic circulation at $15\frac{1}{2}$ to 1, debtors do not want silver *at* or below $15\frac{1}{2}$ to 1, but only below. Their demand will only act on it so long as it stays below; therefore their demand never can lift it again to $15\frac{1}{2}$ to 1. But meanwhile their demand is acting to sustain it only by absorbing any new supply through real purchases. So long, therefore, as there is a new supply, the price must remain below $15\frac{1}{2}$ to 1, and that new supply must be absorbed. But this is destroying the bimetallic and concurrent circulation just so far as it goes on. The bimetallists seem to think that, *if* silver fell, the debtors of the world would all pounce upon it so unanimously and immediately that it would *not* fall. This is absurd in the statement, and it is absurd in every detail of fact. New silver does not rain down in an equal

deposit over the earth. It comes into human society at certain points. Hence the world-wide demand cannot be concentrated on it. Any demand which does act on it can do so only by real transactions under price fluctuations. This fallacy, therefore, reminds us again of perpetual motion, wherein it is believed that we can get effect out of a force without action, reaction, and " escapement."

4. To meet another point somewhat more explicitly than I have done it above, let me say that if any nation which now uses gold finds that its interests are not served thereby, and thinks that silver would serve them better, it has only to make the experiment on its own risk and responsibility. If it succeeds, others will imitate it, and the inferences now made from the past action of nations will have to be modified. So far the nations have always acted as if they knew they were about to commit folly and incur loss whenever they have taken up any projects about silver, and they have insisted on first joining hands so as to all go into the evil together. We wait, then, for the first nation to give up gold and take silver because it thinks silver will serve its interest and convenience better. Mr. Gibbs is as anxious lest England should become a silver nation as any "gold monometallist" possibly could be.

5. If, then, we are asked which nations will take gold and which silver, and why any should take silver, and, if none take silver, where gold enough is to come from, we answer: (1) That it is not possible or necessary to tell *a priori* who will take silver and who gold. (2) All would prefer gold, and the world will probably ultimately come to use only a single universal standard of value, just as it probably will come to use single and universal standards of weights and measures. This, however, is only an anticipation which it must be left to time and the development of civilization to realize. At present it has no importance. If it is a correct anticipation it is fruitless; if it is an incorrect anticipation it is harmless. (3) If it is said that "there is not gold enough," that assertion is senseless unless we add: "to sustain prices and credits at their present level." If, then, there is not enough, in this sense, the nations will compete for gold until those to whom its advantages are worth most get it, because they give most (goods) for it. Others will

drop out of the competition for gold and take silver whenever its comparative cheapness more than counterbalances its inferior utility. So then, if there is not enough gold, we will use silver, and those will take some silver who think it for their interest, all things considered, so to do.

WILLIAM G. SUMNER.

October 25, 1879.

THE ARGUMENT AGAINST PROTECTIVE TAXES.

THE most absurd assertion which can be put into language is that a thing (*e.g.*, free trade) is true in theory but is false in practice. For, if free trade is not true in practice, something else, viz., restricted trade, is alleged to be true and beneficial in practice. It will therefore be a matter of scientific investigation to find out how restriction acts, what forces it brings into action, what are the laws of those forces, what are the conditions of successful restriction, etc. etc.—in short, to find out the theory and philosophy of restriction. The theory thus found will be "true" because deduced from observation and ratified by experience. But it was conceded, at the outset, that free trade is true in theory. Hence it would follow, if free trade is true in theory but not in practice, that two opposite and contradictory propositions about the same subject-matter could both be true at the same time. This is the height of absurdity. Any one, therefore, who makes this assertion is either guilty of very loose thinking, or else he seeks an escape, at all hazards, from rational conclusions against which he can no longer contend.

There remain two possible positions which a protectionist may assume:

1. He may boldly declare that there is a science of wealth based on restriction; that he can discover the principles of it and reduce them to a theory; that trade between countries is a mischievous thing, at least if it runs on parallels of latitude; that isolation and antagonism of nations is the law of nature upon which wealth and civilization depend; that there is therefore no universal science of wealth, but only a national science of wealth, and that this science, in its final analysis, is only a generalization from certain empirical maxims of economic policy. This is the

position of the dogmatic or philosophical protectionists, who seek to give a certain abstract and philosophical cast to their speculations. It is the position of the List-Carey school, whose "unscientific science and unhistorical history" (as Roscher called it) seems to impose with such weight on some people. It is a view of the matter which is especially cultivated now by the learned protectionists of Germany, and which issues in some of the most remarkable curiosities of economic literature which have ever been produced either by the learned or the unlearned.

2. The other ground which the protectionist may take is that protection does not increase wealth, but is, for some reason or other, expedient.

In taking up again now the effort to put into simple, brief, and comprehensive form the argument against protection, I will separate these two modes of defending protection and take them in order. It is obvious that the two positions are inconsistent with each other, and every one who is familiar with the history of this controversy knows that its fruitlessness has been due, in a large measure, to the ambiguities, false definitions, and confusion which have prevailed in it. It has been a constant phenomenon in the discussion that the expediency of protection, in spite of the harm done by it, has been argued, and then the general utility of protection has been assumed as resulting from the argument. I do not know of any disputant on the protectionist side who does not move from one to the other of these positions, as his convenience or the pressure of the argument may force him, or who does not confuse them with each other.

It will be noted also that my point of attack is *protection* under any form or in any degree, and not import duties or taxes on consumption. This distinction can perhaps best be brought out by examining one of the peculiar and whimsical notions which avail to keep people from actually examining the matter in issue, viz., the notion of "revenue tariff with incidental protection." The people who believe that this jingle of words has any meaning in it must believe that the same man in supplying his needs does it at the same time in two ways, by importing and by buying at home too. If A wants a ton of iron and imports it, he pays duties on it which go to the public treasury. Not a cent for this transaction goes to the American producer of iron. This is why the American producer is so often heard to cry out in horror at the amount imported. If B wants a ton of iron and buys it at home, he pays the protective taxes to the home producer, and not a cent goes in revenue to the public treasury for that transaction. What incidental relation exists between these two transactions? They are independent and exclusive of each other. If we discard the empty formula of "revenue with incidental protection," we find that we are simply face to face with the problem of free trade *vs.* protection, or revenue *vs.* protection, as in the first place. Nothing has been done by this formula towards solving either of those problems. A only wanted one ton and took one way of getting it. B only wanted one ton and took another way of getting it. The question why either of them chose the course he did choose, and what the effects were on the interests of either of them, and on the welfare of the country, of the tax laws in question, remains still all before us. What is clear is only that protection and revenue are exclusive of each other. They do not overlap each other at all. The line between them is sharp and precise, and we can discuss the wisdom of protection entirely aside from the wisdom of raising revenue from customs duties. The latter question shall not therefore now be taken into account, and we confine our attention only to the former.

In this connection we may also dispose of another of the glib commonplaces by which people get rid of the trouble of thinking about the tariff controversy: that we have a large debt and therefore must have a high (protective) tariff. It is evident, since protection and revenue exclude each other, that not one cent which is paid in a protective tax goes into the public treasury or helps to pay either the principal or the interest of the debt, while, on the other hand, every cent paid in protective taxes lessens the power of the citizen to pay revenue taxes for the discharge of the public burdens. Hence the fact that we have heavy public burdens is just the reason why we cannot afford to squander our means in paying taxes to our neighbors for carrying on (as they themselves allege) unproductive industries. The especial iniquity of the present tariff, in a political point of view, is that it was laid under the cover of war taxes, taking advantage of the popular ignorance of the relation between protection and revenue, and of the popular willingness to submit to taxation for the purpose of the war. To argue that we want protective taxes because we have a large debt to pay is like arguing that a man ought to squander his income in benevolence because his means are just now being strained by an expensive lawsuit.

Having disposed of these notions which interfere with the approach to the real merits of the question, we may consider first whether protection can increase the wealth of the country.

I. The problem of economic science is presented in the ratio between the efforts which men have to exert to supply their material needs and the amount and excellence of the food, clothing, lodging, furniture, fuel, etc., which they obtain. Political economy investigates the laws which govern this ratio so as to find out how we may determine the ratio as much as possible in our favor. Throwing aside all technicalities, the case is to find out how, for a given exertion and sacrifice, to get the maximum of material good. I maintain against any system of restriction whatsoever that it renders that ratio less favorable to men than it would be under freedom, taking the arts and sciences, the land and the population, as they are in the country where restriction is applied. Instead of increasing wealth, it is mathematically demonstrable that it lessens wealth, makes it harder to get a living and lowers the comfort of the population, and that it does this by taking away one man's earnings to give them to another. I mean to say that a man must work harder and longer to get a given amount of product under protection than under free trade, and I mean to say that this state of things is due to the statute law, which steps in and takes away part of his product and gives it to another man. The issue is purposely stated here without the use of any of the technical terms of political economy, because the simpler and homelier the language is the more correctly does it state the question, both in its economic and its political aspects, both in its scientific and in its popular significance, free from all admixture of either sentimental or pedantic rubbish. The economic question about the tariff is: Does it enable the population of the country to command greater material good for a given effort? The political question about protection is: Does the statute enacted by the legislature alter the distribution of property so that one man enjoys another man's earnings? Has the state a law in operation which enables one citizen to collect taxes of another? The scientific question about protection is: Does it lessen the ratio of effort and sacrifice to comfort and enjoyment? The popular question about protection is: Does it prevent me from supporting myself and family, by my labor, as well as I could do it if there were no protective taxes?

The philosophical protectionists at once reply that this is not the question, or at least not the whole of it. To them political economy is not an independent science. They are not willing to consider the question of wealth aside from other things. They want to embrace in the view what they call moral, political, social, æsthetical, and sentimental considerations. Their instinct is perfectly correct when they oppose those operations of analysis and classification which would introduce clearness and precision into the discussion. The part of social science which has the most positive and mathematical character is the one against which they cannot stand. They write no books on political economy, but always on social science, in order to keep the clear mixed with the unclear, the physical with the metaphysical, the positive with the arbitrary. They are eagerly followed by all the popular orators and writers on economic questions, and generally by those metaphysicians and students of other sciences who take part in sociological discussions, and almost always prove themselves the most reckless dogmatizers when they do so. The attraction of the *a priori* method, and of abstract and general propositions for ill-trained men, is well known, and, generally, in proportion as one is untrained in a particular science (whatever may be his status in others) will be his readiness to fly to *a priori* methods and to dogmas which are conveniently vague, loose, and broad, when he engages in the discussion of questions appertaining to the science in which he has not been trained.

Mr. Carey, for instance, filled his books with vague diatribes about "association." He thought to have found a great principle under this name. He wanted to break off all the natural ties and bonds of mankind in order to piece the parts together again on a plan of his own. He accordingly wrote big books on "social science," and he never reached the first conception of the forces which may truly be called social, or the laws by which they act. He and his school, in this country and in Germany, have never learned to see the great bonds of human society which are developed by intercourse and communication, which hold the nations to a mutual giving and taking as they grow in civilization, which are stronger in proportion as they are natural, informal, impersonal, spontaneous, and in comparison with which all artificial co-operation is ridiculously insignificant. For our present purpose, however, the thing to note is that social speculations and sociological investigations have nothing whatever to do with the tariff for protection. They only obscure and confuse the tariff question. If we should classify them we should find that they are either broader generalizations which flow necessarily from sound economic principles, and so can be left to take care of themselves while the economic investigations are going on ; or else they are sociological doctrines which are parallel with sound economic doctrines, but which are most successfully pursued in special investigations; or else (which is by far the largest class) they are sentimental whims, popular notions, and metaphysical dogmas, which are not true, or at best are only half true, but which cannot be refuted without allowing the discussion to fritter itself away in innumerable side issues. We have to understand that an economic investigation may be carried on just as independently as a chemical or physical or biological investigation. The economist does not need to be on the lookout all the time to correct his results by reference to some outside considerations, or to the dogmas of jejune and rickety systems of metaphysical speculation. On the contrary, he should regard the introduction of extraneous elements, no matter under what high-sounding names, of moral, political, and social, as sure signs of impending confusion and fallacy, and he should especially repel any attempt to measure and criticise his results by the facile generalizations of *a priori* speculation. So much being here briefly set out, we may devote ourselves to the question of protection as a question of wealth and political economy only, as above described.

Let us take the case of a new country. It is claimed that a new country needs protection in order to get a start. Mill seemed to make some concession to this case. I have heard a man who was not a protectionist and who was a professional economist say that he thought a new colony might get into a situation in which it might need a lift to move it on in the way of growth. I will take up this latter view of the matter for discussion because it is the case which, if disproved, will *a fortiori* carry all the other forms of this claim with it.

I pass over the practical difficulty involved in the question who is to decide when the juncture supposed has come about, and who is to prescribe or give the lift; I pass over the unscientific and incorrect conception of econonic forces involved in the hypothesis that a nation can get into any such position, and also in the notion of a "lift" to be given to a nation, in order that I may come to the real test of the remedy proposed, if the case could arise, and if the remedy were practically available. It is evident that a protective tariff cannot render any foreign capital or labor available to help the nation which lays the tariff. If a nation lays import duties for revenue some part of them may fall on the foreigner, but if it lays such duties for protection it keeps foreign goods out. If, then, the foreigner stays at home and is forced to keep his goods at home, the protecting country cannot make use of him or his goods in any way whatever to suit its ends or avert its misfortunes. Whatever effect the protective taxes exert must be exerted in the protecting country, on its own labor and capital. Any favor or encouragement which the protective system exerts on one group of its population must be won by an equivalent oppression exerted on some other group. To suppose the contrary is to deny the most obvious application of the conservation of energy to economic forces. If the legislation did not simply transfer capital it would have to make capital out of nothing. Now the transfer is not simply an equal redistribution; there is loss and waste in the case of any tax whatsoever. There is especial loss and waste in the case of a protective tax. We cannot collect taxes and redistribute them without loss; much less can we produce forced monopolies and distorted industrial relations without loss. It follows then that if a nation could come into some temporary industrial compression or arrested growth, a protective tariff not only would not help it out, but would contribute to still further limit its powers of self-development and to restrain its recuperative energies.

We have then reduced the issue which we are discussing to such terms that, after analyzing the phenomena, we are able to test the protectionist theory by universal canons of science, and we have a mathematical demonstration that protection is a delusion, which, like bimetallism, fiat money, socialism, and utopianism, is an attempt to make something out of nothing, or to create energy by law.

Here we shall be met, however, by the people who insist on believing that a better organization of labor, or greater activity of labor, or some other advantage which is real altho not specific, more than offsets the injury, or that the injured ones participate again in some vague gain. It is very singular that the people who believe in these notions are so slow to understand the fact that whatever lessens the wealth of a community, in the widest generalization or deduction only lessens its wealth! and cannot possibly increase it, and that the result is either to lessen the wealth *per capita*, or, if some do not become poorer, then others must be rendered still more poor. The protective tariff must act on people who without it would distribute their industry according to the chances of the greatest profit. The tariff is needed, by the protectionist hypothesis, in order to counteract the distribution which is thus brought about. But the tariff itself can appeal to no motive save that of desire for profit. It does so by providing that a certain industry shall, under protection, pay higher profits than it could under freedom, and it expects that this inducement will operate to make labor and capital seek this industry. If then desire for profit was not a sufficient and wise guide under freedom, what makes it such under protection? The notion that the legislature has a wisdom greater than that of the people, and can point out the industries they ought to pursue, has often been refuted; but the protective theory really assumes more than that. It assumes that the law can enlighten the desire for profit, and make it a more trustworthy guide than it would be under freedom. In truth there is nothing at all wanted in the cases to which protection is applied but capital, which the law can never produce. The efficiency of the tariff is that it does get this capital—from other people. The rest is all phrases intended to occupy attention while the thimblerig is going on. If this is not so, let some protectionist analyze the operation of his system, and show by reference to undisputed economic principles where and how it exerts any effect on production to increase it. Customs sometimes grow up under the efforts of men to bring about arrangements which will be convenient for industry and commerce. The law can often follow these customs, recognize them, and give them positive form. Institutions grow out of needs, and to meet purposes, to which institutions the law can give form and sanction. I know of nothing more than this which the law can do for industry.

What has been proved now of a new country holds true all the more of an old one. The only difference is that a new country may endure protection while an old one cannot. A new country which produces, as all new countries do, food and raw materials may create parasite industries to live on the exuberant productions of its natural industries, and on the special advantage in exchange which a new country has when it exchanges food and raw materials for finished products. An old country cannot exclude food and raw materials. In a new country the burden of the tariff system falls on the superfluity of the people —superfluity not in respect to what they would like to have, but in comparison with what people in old countries have. In an old country there are large classes of persons who are at best on the verge of poverty, and who are forced to labor hard and for long hours to win subsistence. Taxes on food and raw materials would crush these classes down to misery. Germany is trying it with a tariff which is quite insignificant compared with ours. What I have proved, therefore, with regard to the effect of a protective tariff in a new country holds *a fortiori* in an old country, and is true universally. A restricted trade lowers the physical well-being of the population, and, with that, all chance of intellectual and moral well-being, below what it would be under free trade, with the same conditions of labor, capital, and land.

II. I go on then to consider the other protectionist position : that protection is not a means of wealth, but is temporarily expedient.

Under this head the controversy has rambled over the whole field of economic speculation, embracing also all history and all statistics, and here also the vague sentimental and metaphysical considerations have had the greater scope, as this is the more popular branch of the controversy. I propose to notice only two or three of the arguments for the expediency of the protective tariff, and those I must take more by way of illustration.

During the recent political campaign the chief argument which was used was that the tariff made wages high. I have before me a circular which was widely distributed in which wage-receivers were told that free trade would either force employers to close their shops or to reduce their wages to foreign rates. In Germany the argument is that English workers get higher wages, which proves that they are better workmen, and that the Germans need protection against them. In America the argument is that the Englishmen do not get as good wages as the Americans, and that therefore the Americans need protection. The advantage of an empirical argument is that it goes as well one end foremost as the other. Suppose the Germans should argue like the Americans. They would then have to argue that free trade would *raise* their wages to the English rate, as the Americans argue that free trade would lower *their* wages to the English rate. Suppose the Americans should borrow the German argument. They would then have to argue that, as the Americans get higher wages, it proves that they are better workmen than the English, and need no protection against them, and *a fortiori* none against the workmen of the Continent.

There is one entirely American element in this argument, however. That is the claim or assumption that the high comfort of the American laborers is due to the tariff. One orator during the last campaign, who spoke with the authority of high official position, spoke with contempt and impatience of the low plane on which this tariff question is discussed, as if it were a mere question of dollars and cents, when in fact it is a question of status of the population and of the well-being of the wages classes.

We must distinguish here two propositions about wages which are constantly confused with each other, and which the protectionists find it very useful to confuse, altho they are inconsistent with each other, and both are false.

It is argued (1) that we want protection because wages are high, and (2) that we want protection in order to make wages high. To the legislature the high wages are represented as caused by some independent forces, and as a fact in the condition of the country which constitutes a reason for protection. To the workman it is argued that, the politicians and the employers having considered the matter and agreed that the American workingman ought to be well fed, clothed, etc., they have decided that he must have high wages, and that the tariff is the way to get them for him. This picture of the employers neglecting their business to lobby for a rise in the wages of their own men would be entertaining if it were not really so successful in deceiving those to whom it is addressed. The two branches of this argument about wages demand separate consideration.

1. Sociology is such a new science, and is as yet so little understood, that it is not strange if its doctrines have not yet spread very far through the community, but a superficial acquaintance with it would prevent any one from believing that politicians and statesmen can plan what sort of a people it would please them to have, or what degree of comfort they consider appropriate for the working classes. Nevertheless we have hundreds of politicians and orators who always start from a conception of this sort. It is evident, however, that the people of the United States must get their living out of the soil of the United States. We have an immense amount of land of the best quality, navigable rivers, great forests, mines of metal and coal, and we have to get out what we can with the labor and capital at our disposal. Whatever we get out will be distributed amongst us according to our shares in the production. As the natural stores are very rich and easy to get at, and as the laborers are few, it follows that the average product per laborer is greater than can be obtained in old countries, where the soil is more or less exhausted, and where the population is so dense as to make the competition of life very hard. This latter state of things affords us the second term of comparison by which we measure our status. Taken absolutely, there is plenty of room for improvement in our situation, and in the status of whole classes of our population.

We have, then, a perfectly obvious and sufficient explanation of the status of our people in natural facts. The statesmen have never planned this or done anything to help it. They have only marred it more or less. What we are is the result of our inherited traits and traditions, and of our physical surroundings. What there is about us which is good or bad, strong or weak, is alike to be attributed to these causes. High wages, therefore, or, more properly speaking, high average comfort, with little pauperism or misery, are incidents of our situation as early comers on a new continent. Yet there are people who tell us that they, in their wisdom, have made us well off by taxing us, and that we should not be so well off any more if we should get rid of the taxes, and they persuade the people who pay nearly all the taxes on consumption—namely, the artisans and laborers—that they could not get their living on this continent if they did not pay taxes. That is like telling a laborer who opens his dinner-pail that he would have more dinner if he would throw away a slice of bread.

This continent, however, is not so exclusively favored that it is likely to draw to itself all the population of the globe. Other continents have their advantages, and the one which has the best advantages for food and raw materials cannot in the nature of things have those advantages which come from a dense population and a high development of the arts and sciences. No one will be willing to turn away from the industries for which the country offers the best advantages to take up those in which other countries have the best advantages, unless the difference can be made up to him in some way. Hence manufacturing industry here has always had to contend with the profits possible in agricultural pursuits. Wages—so far as any wages class has ever yet been developed here—must be high enough to give the same scale of comfort as can be won in using land. The high wages and general high average of comfort are, therefore, plainly the same thing, and both proceed together out of the actual physical circumstances of the people.

What, then, can the tariff do about wages? It can only increase the wages in mechanical pursuits by deducting from the gains of agriculture. As we said above, it can win nothing for some without an equivalent or greater deduction from others. It no doubt draws upon each mechanical industry to make it help support all the others, and so it weakens them all; but whatever strength and help it brings to them as a group it must take from other groups. If, then, we are candidly seeking for the true effects of the restrictive system on the national welfare, and on the welfare of special classes, we must note that this operation cannot increase the national welfare, and we must look to see on whom it is that the corresponding loss falls. It is plain that it is upon the agricultural industries of the country, and accordingly a special bundle of fallacies has been devised for deceiving the agriculturists into the belief that they are gainers by it. It is evident, however, that every reduction in agricultural profits makes it easier for the employer to compete with the land for labor. The rising wages and the falling profits of agriculture meet each other at a point below what the profits of agriculture would be under freedom. If there were no tariff, the wages of the wages class must go up to the full measure of the agricultural profits under freedom. Hence the tariff lowers wages. It never has had and never can have any other effect. The employer in a protected industry pays no more than market rates for wages, and he could not possibly pay any less. The notion that he could lower wages to some foreign level in the midst of a country where labor could win higher rewards is of course absurd.

We see, then, that the argument that the tariff makes wages high is entirely without foundation. It has lowered wages. We see that the notion of having a tariff in order to secure to our people what they have as their birthright, and what the tariff only diminishes, viz., a comparatively better and easier existence than the people of older countries, is an imposture. It has very great popular effect because the popular notion is generally that we owe all our prosperity to ourselves and to what we call "our institutions," when in truth we owe everything that we are to historical antecedents and physical conditions.

Having stripped off this humbug from the issue, as stated by the protectionists, we may come back to the scornful complaint that we are discussing the question on a low level. We were told that we ought to debate it as a great question of status of the population, etc., and we have found that this was all rhetoric and fustian except the effect of the tariff to lower the status of the population. It follows, then, that we were right to debate it as a question of dollars and cents only. There is nothing else in it. A wants protection; that is, he wants B's money. B does not want to let him have it. A talks sentiment and metaphysics finely, and, after all, all there is in it is that he wants B's money. A does not otherwise show much interest in sentiment and patriotism and metaphysical goods generally. He never goes to Washington to lobby for education, or scientific research, or geographical exploration, or for any philanthropic scheme, unless there is a chance in it for him to get B's money. He is then moved to scorn at B's sordid love of money, and he goes to hear a lecture on "materialism" to gratify his wounded feelings because B will not give up his money. The matter is all stated from A's standpoint. We see him all the time. For him to want B's money is patriotic. It is "developing our resources." It is noble. For B to want to keep the same money is mean. I insist upon the matter being stated in the most crass and vulgar way, just because that is all there is of it when the humbug is all eliminated. The student of history then recognizes a very old friend. The robber-barons, Robin Hood, Dick Turpin, and others have had the same opinion of the nobility of wanting other people's money, and of the meanness of the "trader" or laborer who did not want to lose his earnings.

2. Let us next look at the other doctrine, that we need a protective tariff because wages are high; or the equivalent doctrine, that we cannot compete. The people of the United States can compete with anybody in getting wealth. The high wages are a proof of it; but they cannot compete with everybody else in every form of industry. They have only a limited number of laborers and a limited amount of capital. The same man cannot be doing two things at once. The same capital cannot be employed in two uses. Hence it will be wise and necessary to choose the *most* profitable of all the profitable employments which are possible. It will follow that we cannot afford to compete in any industry which will not pay here as well as those which have special advantages here. If we cannot compete, it is because we cannot afford to compete. We are too well off. We cannot compete with "foreign paupers," just because we are not paupers. "Pauper," of course, is one of those silly and invidious terms which have been introduced into this discussion in the interest of falsehood and folly. Paupers and

princes live in idleness supported by taxation. No one can compete with them. Seriously, then, we cannot compete with men who are fiercely competing with each other for low wages in a dense population because we are not fiercely competing with each other. We have abundant chances. The protectionists are not content, however, to use our advantages and avoid competition, which is what every sensible man does in private life. According to them we must go to seek competition. It will be told in history that a public bureau of our government spent part of the capital of the nation in seeking competition with Chinamen in making tea, at the very moment when the same government was trying to devise means to prevent Chinese competition in this country, where it could do no harm. As we shall seek competition with less favorably situated people only at a constant loss as compared with the gains we might win in our own favored industries, those who are carrying on the self-supporting industries must pay taxes to make up the loss, and the wealth of the country must undergo a constant waste. If a blacksmith should say that he could not compete with the shoemaker at making shoes, and therefore that he ought to be paid twice as much as the shoemaker for making shoes, his sanity would be doubted, but that is just the argument that we need a tariff because wages are high. It is because wages are high that we do not need one, and it is because we cannot compete in certain industries that we ought not to try. Some people think it is derogatory to us not to do everything for ourselves; and as they always seem glad to hear that we are exporting more and more, they seem to be desirous that we should make things for all the rest of the world too. What, then, I ask, is the rest of the world to do for us? If we take all the industries, how will they pay us for what we do for them? Competition is the force which under freedom indicates to us what we can do for ourselves and them, and what we can let them do for us to our final maximum advantage. To shut off competition and go into the industries which the ignorant empiricism of Congress or. the caprice of individuals may select, is like unhinging the compass and steering the ship by chance.

3. There is no argument for the expediency of the tariff to be found in the matter of wages in any of its aspects, but it is

sometimes claimed that it is expedient to force certain industries into existence. This is called "developing our industries." We are good-natured enough to call them " our" industries, perhaps because we all pay taxes to support them, not because we own stock in them or participate in the profits. There is a very strong popular notion that it is a good thing for A, B, and C that there should be certain mills, factories, etc., up and down the country—a notion which has no support in fact at all, unless A, B, and C are owners of land near the factories, etc. If an individual were shown statistics of men employed, wages, capital, plant, output, etc., of a certain establishment, and were asked to invest in it, he would no doubt inquire, after all, whether the establishment made profits, since unfortunately not every big chimney does so; but when we are making speeches or writing essays about tariff, this last question is entirely ignored, and big figures and exclamation-points take the place of the only question which is important. If an industry does not pay, it is an industrial abomination. It is wasting and destroying. The larger it is the more mischief it does. The protected manufacturer is forced to allege, when he asks for protection, that his business would not pay without it. He proposes to waste capital. If he should waste his own wealth he would not go on long. He therefore asks the legislature to give him power to lay taxes on his fellow-citizens, to collect from them the capital which he intends to waste, and good wages for himself while he is carrying on that business besides. This is what is called " developing our industries," and the operation of the law is such that the waste and destruction can go on indefinitely. Either an industry can pay under freedom, in which case it does not need protection, or else it would not pay under freedom, in which case it is wasting the wealth of the nation as long as it goes on. It follows that the protective tariff is not a temporary expedient, and it is mathematically impossible that it should ever issue in an independent and productive industry. Other forces may come into play in time, viz., those which would at that time have called the industry in question into existence, and these forces may render the industry independent, but the tariff can never produce any such result.

4. Some have believed that the tariff system brought capital

into the country, and two or three instances of foreign manufacturers who have established branches here have been pointed to as triumphant proofs of it. I know of no statistics either of the amount of capital so imported or of the amount which the tariff has caused to be exported; but I should judge from such information as I have that one just about equalled the other. What is far more important, however, is that if the tariff were taken off any one of a great number of important articles, the people could save more capital in a month out of their diminished cost of living than all the capital which has been brought in here in twenty years on account of the tariff. A similar observation applies to the argument for deferring the reform of the tariff, that it would destroy capital now invested. No one proposes or desires any reckless action which would disregard vested interests of any kind, altho I do not see what difference it would make with what any one would really *do*, whether he had warning that the tariff would be repealed in five years or in five days, but that is a question for a statesman, and not for an economist. The economist may point out that, if any capital were destroyed, the savings of the people from a diminished cost of living would constitute an enormous fund for replacing that capital and offsetting that loss, so that, as far as the mere loss of capital is concerned, there would be no argument for delay.

5. I proceed to a brief but very cogent argument why a protective tariff is not expedient. Protection works all the time against improvement. In April, 1838, New York City indulged in great rejoicings over the arrival of the first steamships from Europe. In April, 1842, at an "Industrial Convention" held in New York City, the opening of steam navigation on the ocean was alleged as one of the chief arguments for protection. We are taxed to open our rivers and harbors, and the result is cheaper goods. That is the benefit which we anticipated and were working for, thinking that it would be a gain. As soon as it is realized, however, comes a clamor from home-producers of those kinds of goods which have been cheapened. "What! Do you mean to say that it is a good thing for the country to have people get the things which we make at a low price? This will never do;" and so a tax-barrier is set up across the rivers

and harbors to imitate the former barrier of sand and rock, and make things as dear.and as hard to get as before. If protection is expedient, then this argument is sound, and we need more protection the more our communication with foreign nations is facilitated. Steamships, ocean cables, and cheap newspapers are all the time neutralizing the existing protection, and more taxes are necessary to give the same protection. If protection is sound, then those who rejoice over improvements in communication and transportation and support protection are guilty of absurd folly. If improvements, inventions, and discoveries are real benefits to mankind, then protection is inexpedient as well as philosophically absurd.

Commerce is plainly entering on a new stage. Common-sense makes its way very slowly into the minds of men when it has to rely on its own merits, but the course of progress in industry and commerce is such that self-interest often becomes hand-maid to common-sense, and then common-sense gets a chance. We have seen five or six new industries grow up in this country within a few years. They are all "land" industries; that is, they belong to the natural advantages of the country. They are in their infancy, but they are already great, and what they are to become no one can guess. They depend on a foreign market, and they have been made possible by cheap and quick ocean transit. Within a year a fleet of new steamers promises new growth in the same direction. The internal transportation of the country, especially in the West and South-west, will support the same growth. The effect is to cause great changes in the distribution of labor, great absorptions of capital in new orders of investments, and the creation of immense new interests. It would be overbold to predict specific results, but this much is clear: the competition of American agriculture will drive English labor and capital more exclusively into manufacturing and commerce. The complementary effect must be exerted here, and the profits of land industries will draw off labor and capital from manufactures and commerce. In other words, the international division of labor will be rendered more perfect, and the consequence must be greater wealth for all. But if the tariff still remains as a barrier to imports, *i.e.*, return cargoes, the exchanges must rule low to the detriment of all the exporting interests, and if specie is imported prices must advance. But the exports cannot rise, since they are forced to seek a foreign market. They will therefore be low, while everything else inside the country is high. This is, of course, the operation of the tariff now all the time, and it is the mode in which the tariff oppresses the land industries; but the whole course of the development which I am anticipating will be to make this oppression harder and sharper, while the tariff will all the time need to be raised higher and higher if it is to be of any avail at all. How long will the system stand such a double strain? If there is any industry which really depends upon the tariff, it cannot too soon begin to learn to do without it.

WILLIAM G. SUMNER.

November, 1881.

SOCIOLOGY.

EACH of the sciences which, by giving to man greater knowledge of the laws of nature, has enabled him to cope more intelligently with the ills of life, has had to fight for its independence of metaphysics. We have still lectures on metaphysical biology in some of our colleges and in some of our public courses, but biology has substantially won its independence. Anthropology is more likely to give laws to metaphysics than to accept laws from that authority. Sociology, however, the latest of this series of sciences, is rather entering upon the struggle than emerging from it. Sociology threatens to withdraw an immense range of subjects of the first importance from the dominion of *a priori* speculation and arbitrary dogmatism, and the struggle will be severe in proportion to the dignity and importance of the subject. The struggle, however, is best carried forward indirectly, by simply defining the scope of sociology, and by vindicating its position amongst the sciences, while leaving its relations to the other sciences and other pursuits of men to adjust themselves according to the facts. I know of nothing more amusing in these days than to see an old-fashioned metaphysician applying his tests to the results of scientific investigation, and screaming with rage because men of scientific training do not care whether the results satisfy those tests or not.

Sociology is the science of life in society. It investigates the forces which come into action wherever a human society exists. It studies the structure and functions of the organs of human society, and its aim is to find out the laws[1] in subordi-

[1] It has been objected that no proof is offered that social laws exist in the order of nature. By what demonstration could any such proof be given *a priori*? If a

nation to which human society takes its various forms, and social institutions grow and change. Its practical utility consists in deriving the rules of right social living from the facts and laws which prevail by nature in the constitution and functions of society. It must, without doubt, come into collision with all other theories of right living which are founded on authority, tradition, arbitrary invention, or poetic imagination.

Sociology is perhaps the most complicated of all the sciences, yet there is no domain of human interest the details of which are treated ordinarily with greater facility. Various religions have various theories of social living, which they offer as authoritative and final. It has never, so far as I know, been asserted by anybody that a man of religious faith (in any religion) could not study sociology or recognize the existence of any such science; but it is incontestably plain that a man who accepts the dogmas about social living which are imposed by the authority of any religion must regard the subject of right social living as settled and closed, and he cannot enter on any investigation the first groundwork of which would be doubt of the authority which he recognizes as final. Hence social problems and social phenomena present no difficulty to him who has only to cite an authority or obey a prescription.

Then again the novelists set forth "views" about social matters. To write and read novels is perhaps the most royal road to teaching and learning which has ever been devised. The proceeding of the novelists is kaleidoscopic. They turn the same old bits of colored glass over and over again into new combinations. There is no limit, no sequence, no bond of consistency. The romance-writing social philosopher always proves his case just as a man always wins who plays chess with himself.

Then again the utopians and socialists make easy work of the complicated phenomena with which sociology has to deal. These persons, vexed with the intricacies of social problems, and revolting against the facts of the social order, take upon themselves the task of inventing a new and better world.

man of scientific training finds his attention arrested, in some group of phenomena, by those sequences, relations, and recurrences which he has learned to note as signs of action of law, he seeks to discover the law. If it exists, he finds it. What other proof of its existence could there be?

They brush away all which troubles us men, and create a world free from annoying limitations and conditions—in their imagination. In ancient times, and now in half-civilized countries, these persons have been founders of religions. Something of that type always lingers around them still and among us, and is to be seen amongst the reformers and philanthropists who never contribute much to the improvement of society in any actual detail, but find a key principle for making the world anew and regenerating society. I have even seen faint signs of the same mysticism in social matters in some of the greenbackers who have "thought out" in bed, as they relate, a scheme of wealth by paper money, as Mahomet would have received a Surah, or Joe Smith a revelation about polygamy. Still there are limits to this resemblance, because in our nineteenth-century American life a sense of humor, even if defective, answers some of the purposes of common-sense.

Then again all the whimsical people who have hobbies of one sort or another, and who cluster around the Social Science Association, come forward with projects which are the result of a strong impression, an individual misfortune, or an unregulated benevolent desire, and which are therefore the product of a facile emotion, not of a laborious investigation.

Then again the *dilettanti* make light work of social questions. Every one, by the fact of living in society, gathers some observations of social phenomena. The belief grows up, as it was expressed some time ago by a professor of mathematics, that everybody knows about the topics of sociology. Those topics have a broad and generous character. They lend themselves easily to generalizations. There are as yet no sharp tests formulated. Above all, and worst lack of all as yet, we have no competent criticism. Hence it is easy for the aspirant after culture to venture on this field without great danger of being brought to account, as he would be if he attempted geology, or physics, or biology. Even a scientific man of high attainments in some other science, in which he well understands what special care, skill, and training are required, will not hesitate to dogmatize about a topic of sociology. A group of half-educated men may be relied upon to attack a social question and to hammer it dead in a few minutes with a couple of commonplaces and a sweeping *a priori* assumption. Above all other topics, social topics lend themselves to the purposes of the diner-out.

Two facts, however, in regard to social phenomena need only be mentioned to be recognized as true. (1) Social phenomena always present themselves to us in very complex combinations, and (2) it is by no means easy to interpret the phenomena. The phenomena are often at three or four removes from their causes. Tradition, prejudice, fashion, habit, and other similar obstacles continually warp and deflect the social forces, and they constitute interferences whose magnitude is to be ascertained separately for each case. It is also impossible for us to set up a social experiment. To do that, we should need to dispose of the time and liberty of a certain number of men. It follows that sociology requires a special method, and that probably no science requires such peculiar skill and sagacity in the observer and interpreter of the phenomena which are to be studied. One peculiarity may be especially noted because it shows a very common error of students of social science. A sociologist needs to arrange his facts before he has obtained them; that is to say, he must make a previous classification so as to take up the facts in a certain order. If he does not do this he may be overwhelmed in the mass of his material so that he never can master it. How shall any one know how to classify until the science itself has made some progress? Statistics furnish us the best illustration at the present time of the difficulty here referred to.

When, now, we take into account these difficulties and requirements, it is evident that the task of sociology is one which will call for especial and long training, and that it will probably be a long time yet before we can train up any body of special students who will be so well trained in the theory and science of society as to be able to form valuable opinions on points of social disease and social remedy. But it is a fact of familiar observation that all popular discussions of social questions seize directly upon points of social disease and social remedies. The diagnosis of some asserted social ill and the prescription of the remedy are undertaken offhand by the first comer, and without reflecting that the diagnosis of a social disease is many times harder than that of a disease in an individual, and that to prescribe for a society is to prescribe for an organism which is immortal. To err in prescribing for a man is at worst to kill him; to err in prescribing for a society is to set in operation injurious forces which extend, ramify, and multiply their effects in ever new combinations throughout an indefinite future. It may pay to experiment with an individual because he cannot wait for medical science to be perfected; it cannot pay to experiment with a society because the society does not die and can afford to wait.

If we have to consider the need of sociology, innumerable reasons for studying it present themselves. In spite of all our acquisitions in natural science, the conception of a natural law (which is the most important good to be won from studying natural science) is yet exceedingly vague in the minds of ordinary intelligent people, and is very imperfect even amongst the educated. That conception is hardly yet applied by anybody to social facts and problems. Social questions force themselves upon us in multitudes every year as our civilization advances and our society becomes complex. When such questions arise they are wrangled over and tossed about without any orderly discussion, but as if they were only the sport of arbitrary whims. Is it not then necessary that we enable ourselves, by study of the facts and laws of society, to take up such questions from the correct point of view, and to proceed with the examination of them in such order and method that we can reach solid results, and thus obtain command of an increasing mass of knowledge about social phenomena? The assumption which underlies almost all discussion of social topics is that we men need only make up our minds what kind of a society we want to have, and that then we can devise means for calling that society into existence. It is assumed that we can decide to live on one spot of the earth's surface or another, and to pursue there one industry or another, and then that we can, by our devices, make that industry as productive as any other could be in that place. People believe that we have only to choose whether we will have aristocratic institutions or democratic institutions. It is believed that statesmen can, if they will, put a people in the way of material prosperity. It is believed that rent on land can be abolished if it is not thought expedient to have it. It is assumed that peasant proprietors can be brought into existence anywhere where it is thought that it would be an advantage to have them. These illustrations might be multiplied indefinitely. They show the need of sociology, and if we should go on to notice the general conceptions of society, its ills and their remedies, which are held by various religious, political, and social sects, we should find ample further evidence of the need of sociology.

Let us then endeavor to define the field of sociology. Life in society is the life of a human society on this earth. Its elementary conditions are set by the nature of human beings and the nature of the earth. We have already become familiar, in biology, with the transcendent importance of the fact that life on earth must be maintained by a struggle against nature, and also by a competition with other forms of life. In the latter fact biology and sociology touch. Sociology is a science which deals with one range of phenomena produced by the struggle for existence, while biology deals with another. The forces are the same, acting on different fields and under different conditions. The sciences are truly cognate. Nature contains certain materials which are capable of satisfying human needs, but those materials must, with rare and mean exceptions, be won by labor, and must be fitted to human use by more labor. As soon as any number of human beings are each struggling to win from nature the material goods necessary to support life, and are carrying on this struggle side by side, certain social forces come into operation. The prime condition of this society will lie in the ratio of its numbers to the supply of materials within its reach. For the supply at any moment attainable is an exact quantity, and the number of persons who can be supplied is arithmetically limited. If the actual number present is very much less than the number who might be supported, the condition of all must be ample and easy. Freedom and facility mark all social relations under such a state of things. If the number is larger than that which can be supplied, the condition of all must be one of want and distress, or else a few must be well provided, the others being proportionately still worse off. Constraint, anxiety, possibly tyranny and repression mark social relations. It is when the social pressure due to an unfavorable ratio of population to land becomes intense that the social forces develop increased activity. Division of labor, exchange, higher social organization, emigration, advance in the arts, spring from the necessity of contending against the harsher conditions of existence which are continually reproduced as the population surpasses the means of existence on any given status.

The society with which we have to deal does not consist of any number of men. An army is not a society. A man with his wife and his children constitutes a society, for its essential parts are all present, and the number more or less is immaterial. A certain division of labor between the sexes is imposed by nature. The family as a whole maintains itself better under an organization with division of labor than it could if the functions were shared so far as possible. From this germ the development of society goes on by the regular steps of advancement to higher organization, accompanied and sustained by improvements in the arts. The increase of population goes on according to biological laws which are capable of multiplying the species beyond any assignable limits, so that the number to be provided for steadily advances, and the status of ease and abundance gives way to a status of want and constraint. Emigration is the first and simplest remedy. By winning more land the ratio of population to land is once more rendered favorable. It is to be noticed, however, that emigration is painful to all men. To the uncivilized man, to emigrate means to abandon a mass of experiences and traditions which have been won by suffering, and to go out to confront new hardships and perils. To the civilized man migration means cutting off old ties of kin and country. The earth has been peopled by man at the cost of this suffering.

On the side of the land also stands the law of the diminishing return as a limitation. More labor gets more from the land, but not proportionately more. Hence, if more men are to be supported, there is need not of a proportionate increase of labor, but of a disproportionate increase of labor. The law of population, therefore, combined with the law of the diminishing return constitutes the great underlying condition of society. Emigration, improvements in the arts, in morals, in education, in political organization, are only stages in the struggle of man to meet these conditions, to break their force for a time, and to win room under them for ease and enlargement. Ease and enlargement mean either power to support more men on a given stage of comfort or power to advance the comfort of a given number of men. Progress is a word which has no meaning save in view of the laws of population and the diminishing return, and it is quite natural that any one who fails to understand those laws should fall into doubt which way progress points, whether towards wealth or poverty. The laws of population and the diminishing return, in their combination, are the iron spur which has driven the race on to all which. it has ever achieved, and the fact that population ever advances, yet advances against a barrier which resists more stubbornly at every step of advance, unless it is removed to a new distance by some conquest of man over nature, is the guarantee that the task of civilization will never be ended, but that the need for more energy, more intelligence, and more virtue will never cease while the race lasts. If it were possible for an increasing population to be sustained by proportionate increments of labor, we should all still be living in the original home of the race on the spontaneous products of the earth. Let him, therefore, who desires to study social phenomena first learn the transcendent importance for the whole social organization, industrial, political, and civil, of the ratio of population to land.

We have noticed that the relations involved in the struggle for existence are two-fold. There is first the struggle of individuals to win the means of subsistence from nature, and secondly there is the competition of man with man in the effort to win a limited supply. The radical error of the socialists and sentimentalists is that they never distinguish these two relations from each other. They bring forward complaints which are really to be made, if at all, against the author of the universe for the hardships which man has to endure in his struggle with nature. The complaints are addressed, however, to society; that is, to other men under the same hardships. The only social element, however, is the competition of life, and when society is blamed for the ills which belong to the human lot, it is only burdening those who have successfully contended with those ills with the further task of conquering the same ills over again for somebody else. Hence liberty perishes in all socialistic schemes, and the tendency of such schemes is to the deterioration of society by burdening the good members and relieving the bad ones. The law of the survival of the fittest was not made by man and cannot be abrogated by man. We can only, by interfering with it, produce the survival of the unfittest. If a man comes forward with any grievance against the order of society so far as this is shaped by human agency, he must have patient hearing and full redress; but if he addresses a demand to society for relief from the hardships of life, he asks simply that somebody else should get his living for him. In that case he ought to be left to find out his error from hard experience.

The sentimental philosophy starts from the first principle that nothing is true which is disagreeable, and that we must not believe anything which is "shocking" no matter what the evidence may be. There are various stages of this philosophy. It touches on one side the intuitional philosophy which proves that certain things must exist by proving that man needs them, and it touches on the other side the vulgar socialism which affirms that the individual has a right to whatever he needs, and that this right is good against his fellowmen. To this philosophy in all its grades the laws of population and the diminishing return have always been very distasteful. The laws which entail upon mankind an inheritance of labor cannot be acceptable to any philosophy which maintains that man comes into the world endowed with natural rights, and an inheritor of freedom. It is a death-blow to any intuitional philosophy to find out, as an historical fact, what diverse thoughts, beliefs, and actions man has manifested, and it requires but little actual knowledge of human history to show that the human race has never had any ease which it did not earn, or any freedom which it did not conquer. Sociology, therefore, by the investigations which it pursues dispels illusions about what society is or may be, and gives instead knowledge of facts which are the basis of intelligent effort by man to make the best of his circumstances on earth. Sociology, therefore, which can never accomplish anything more than to enable us to make the best of our situation, will never be able to reconcile itself with those philosophies which are trying to find out how we may arrange things so as to satisfy any ideal of society.

The competition of life has taken the form, historically, of a struggle for the possession of the soil. In the simpler states of society the possession of the soil is tribal, and the struggles take place between groups, producing the wars and feuds which constitute almost the whole of early history. On the agricultural stage the tribal or communal possession of land exists as a survival, but it gives way to private property in land whenever the community advances and the institutions are free to mould themselves. The agricultural stage breaks up tribal relations and encourages individualization. This is one of the reasons why it is such an immeasurable advance over the lower forms of civilization. It sets free individual energy, and, while the social bond gains in scope and variety, it also gains in elasticity, for the solidarity of the group is broken up, and the individual may work out his own ends by his own means, subject only to the social ties which lie in the natural conditions of human life. It is only on the agricultural stage that liberty as civilized men understand it exists at all. The poets and sentimentalists, untaught to recognize the grand and world-wide co-operation which is secured by the free play of individual energy under the great laws of the social order, bewail the decay of early communal relations, and exalt the liberty of the primitive stages of civilization. These notions all perish at the first touch of actual investigation. The whole retrospect of human history runs downwards towards beast-like misery and slavery to the destructive forces of nature. The whole history has been one series of toilsome, painful, and bloody struggles, first to find out where we were and what were the conditions of greater ease, and then to devise means to get relief. Most of the way the motives of advance have been experience of suffering and instinct. It is only in the most recent years that science has undertaken to teach without and in advance of suffering, and as yet science has to fight so hard against tradition that its authority is only slowly winning recognition. The institutions whose growth constitutes the advance of civilization have their guarantee in the very fact that they grew and became established. They suited man's purpose better than what went before. They are all imperfect, and all carry with them incidental ills, but each came to be because it was better than what went before, and each which has perished perished because a better one supplanted it.

It follows once and for all that to turn back to any defunct institution or organization because existing institutions are imperfect is to turn away from advance and is to retrograde. The path of improvement lies forwards. Private property in land, for instance, is an institution which has been developed in the most direct and legitimate manner. It may give way at a future time to some other institution which will grow up by imperceptible stages out of the efforts of men to contend successfully with existing evils, but the grounds for private property in land are easily perceived, and it is safe to say that no *a priori* scheme of state ownership or other tenure invented *en bloc* by any philosopher and adopted by legislative act will ever supplant it. To talk of any such thing is to manifest a total misconception of the facts and laws which it is the province of sociology to investigate. The case is less in magnitude but scarcely less out of joint with all correct principle when it is proposed to adopt a unique tax on land, in a country where the rent of land is so low that any important tax on land exceeds it, and therefore becomes indirect, and where also political power is in the hands of small landowners, who hold (without ever having formulated it) a doctrine of absolute property in the soil such as is not held by any other landowners in the world.

Sociology must exert a most important influence on political economy. Political economy is the science which investigates the laws of the material welfare of human societies. It is not its province to teach individuals how to get rich. It is a social science. It was the first branch of sociology which was pursued by man as a science. It is not strange that when the industrial organization of society was studied apart from the organism of which it forms a part it was largely dominated over by arbitrary dogmatism, and that it should have fallen into disrepute as a mere field of opinion, and of endless wrangling about opinions for which no guarantees could be given. The rise of a school of "historical" economists is itself a sign of a struggle towards a positive and scientific study of political economy, in its due relations to other social sciences, and this sign loses none of its significance in spite of the crudeness and extravagance of the opinions of the historical economists, and in spite of their very marked tendency to fall into dogmatism and hobby-riding. Political economy is thrown overboard by all groups and persons whenever it becomes troublesome. When it got in the way of Mr. Gladstone's land-bill he relegated it, by implication, to the planet Saturn, to the great delight of all the fair-traders, protectionists, soft-money men, and others who had found it in the way of their devices. What political economy needs in order to emerge from the tangle in which it it is now involved, and to win a dignified and orderly development, is to find its field and its relations to other sciences fairly defined within the wider scope of sociology. Its laws will then take their place not as arbitrary or broken fragments, but in due relation to other laws. Those laws will win proof and establishment from this relation.

For instance: We have plenty of books, some of them by able writers, in which the old-fashioned Malthusian doctrine of population and the Ricardian law of rent are disputed because emigration, advance in the arts, etc. etc., can offset the action of those laws, or because those laws are not seen in action in the United States. Obviously no such objections ever could have been raised if the laws in question had been understood or had been put in their proper bearings. The Malthusian law of population and the Ricardian law of rent are cases in which, by rare and most admirable acumen, powerful thinkers perceived two great laws in particular phases of their action. With wider information it now appears that the law of population breaks the barriers of Malthus' narrower formulæ and appears as a great law of biology. The Ricardian law of rent is only a particular application of one of the great conditions of production. We have before us not special dogmas of political economy, but facts of the widest significance for the whole social development of the race. To object that these facts may be set aside by migration or advance in the arts is nothing to the purpose, for this is only altering the constants in the equation, which does not alter the form of the curve, but only its position relatively to some standard line. Furthermore, the laws themselves indicate that they have a maximum point for any society, or any given stage of the arts, and a condition of under-population, or of an extractive industry below its maximum, is just as consistent with the law as a condition of over-population and increasing distress. Hence inferences as to the law of population drawn from the status of an under-populated country are sure to be fallacious. In like manner arguments drawn from American phenomena in regard to rent and wages, when rent and wages are as yet only very imperfectly developed here, lead to erroneous conclusions. It only illustrates the unsatisfactory condition of political economy, and the want of strong criticism in it, that such arguments can find admission to its discussions and disturb its growth.

It is to the pursuit of sociology and the study of the industrial organization in combination with the other organizations of society that we must look for the more fruitful development of political economy. We are already in such a position with sociology that a person who has gained what we now possess of that science will bring to bear upon economic problems a sounder judgment and a more correct conception of all social relations than a person who may have read a library of the existing treatises on political economy. The essential elements of political economy are only corollaries or special cases of sociological principles. One who has command of the law of the conservation of energy as it manifests itself in society is armed at once against socialism, protectionism, paper money, and a score of other economic fallacies. The sociological view of political economy also includes whatever is sound in the dogmas of the "historical school," and furnishes what that school is apparently groping after.

As an illustration of the light which sociology throws on a great number of political and social phenomena which are constantly misconstrued, we may notice the differences in the industrial, political, and civil organization which are produced all along at different stages of the ratio of population to land.

When a country is under-populated new-comers are not competitors but assistants. If more come they may produce not only new quotas, but a surplus besides, to be divided between themselves and all who were present before. In such a state of things land is abundant and cheap. The possession of it confers no power or privilege. No one will work for another for wages when he can take up new land and be his own master. Hence it will pay no one to own more land than he can cultivate by his own labor, or with such aid as his own family supplies. Hence, again, land bears little or no rent, there will be no landlords living on rent, and no laborers living on wages, but only a middle class of yeoman farmers. All are substantially on an equality, and democracy becomes the political form, because this is the only state of society in which the dogmatic assumption of equality, on which democracy is based, is realized as a fact. The same effects are powerfully re-enforced by other facts. In a new and under-populated country the industries which are most profitable are the extractive industries. The characteristic of these, with the exception of some kinds of mining, is that they call for only a low organization of labor and small amount of capital. Hence they allow the workman to become speedily his own master, and they educate him to freedom, independence, and self-reliance. At the same time, the social groups being only vaguely marked off from each other, it is easy to pass from one class of occupations, and consequently from one social grade, to another. Finally, under the same circumstances, education, skill, and superior training have but inferior value compared with what they have in densely populated countries. The advantages lie, in an under-populated country, with the coarser, unskilled, manual occupations, and not with the highest developments of science, literature, and art.

If now we turn for comparison to cases of over-population we see that the struggle for existence and the competition of life are intense where the pressure of population is great. This competition draws out the highest achievements. It makes the advantages of capital, education, talent, skill, and training tell to the utmost. It draws out the social scale upwards and downwards to great extremes, and produces aristocratic social organizations in spite of all dogmas of equality. Landlords, tenants (*i.e.*, capitalist employers), and laborers are the three primary divisions of any aristocratic order, and they are sure to be developed whenever land bears rent, and whenever tillage requires the application of large capital. At the same time liberty has to undergo curtailment. A man who has a square mile to himself can easily do as he likes, but a man who walks Broadway at noon or lives in a tenement-house finds his power to do as he likes limited by scores of considerations for the rights and feelings of his fellow-men. Furthermore, organization with subordination and discipline is essential in order that the society as a whole may win a support from the land. In an over-populated country the extremes of wealth and luxury are presented side by side with the extremes of poverty and distress. They are equally the products of an intense social pressure. The achievements of power are highest, the rewards of prudence, energy, enterprise, foresight, sagacity, and all other industrial virtues is greatest ; on the other hand, the penalties of folly, weakness, error, and vice are most terrible. Pauperism, prostitution, and crime are the attendants of a state of society in which science, art, and literature reach their highest developments. Now it is evident that over-population and under-population are only relative terms. Hence as time goes on any under-populated nation is surely moving forward towards the other status, and is speedily losing its natural advantages which are absolute, and also that relative advantage which belongs to it if it is in neighborly relations with nations of dense population and high civilization, viz., the chance to borrow and assimilate from them the products, in arts and science, of high civilization, without enduring the penalties of intense social pressure.

We have seen that if we should try by any measures of arbitrary interference and relief to relieve the victims of social pressure from the calamity of their position, we should only offer premiums to folly and vice and extend them further. We have also seen that we must go forward and meet our problems. We cannot escape them by running away. If then it be asked what the wit and effort of man can do to struggle with the problems offered by social pressure, the answer is that he can do only what his instinct has correctly and surely led him to do without any artificial social organization of any kind, and that is, by improvements in the arts, in science, in morals, in political institutions, to widen and strengthen the power of man over nature. The task of dealing with social ills is not a new task. People set about it and discuss it as if the human race had hitherto neglected it, and as if the solution of the problem was to be something new in form and substance, different from the solution of all problems which have hitherto engaged human effort. In truth, the human race has never done anything else but struggle with the problem of social welfare. That struggle constitutes history, or the life of the human race on earth. That struggle embraces all minor problems which occupy human attention here, save those of religion, which reaches beyond this world and finds its objects beyond this life. Every successful effort to widen the power of man over nature is a real victory over poverty, vice, and misery, taking things in general and in the long-run. It would be hard to find a single instance of a direct assault by positive effort upon poverty, vice, and misery which has not either failed or, if it has not failed directly and entirely, has not entailed other evils greater than the one which it removed. The only two things which really tell on the welfare of man on earth are hard work and self-denial (*i.e.*, in technical language, labor and capital), and these tell most when they are brought to bear directly upon the effort to earn an honest living, to accumulate capital, and to bring up a family of children to be industrious and self-denying in their turn. I repeat that this is the way to work for the welfare of man on earth ; and what I mean to say is that the common notion that when we are going to work for the social welfare of man we must adopt a great dogma, organize for the realization of some great scheme, have before us an abstract ideal, or otherwise do anything but live honest and industrious lives, is a great mistake. From the stand-point of the sociologist pessimism and optimism are alike impertinent. To be an optimist one must forget the frightful sanctions which are attached to the laws of right living. To be a pessimist one must overlook the education and growth which are the product of effort and self-denial. In either case one is passing judgment on what is inevitably fixed, and on which the approval or condemnation of man can produce no effect. The facts and laws are, once and for all, so, and for us men that is the end of the matter. The only persons for whom there would be any sense in the question whether life is worth living are primarily the yet unborn children, and secondarily the persons who are proposing to found families. For these latter the question would take a somewhat modified form: Will life be worth living for children born of me? This question is, unfortunately, not put to themselves by the appropriate persons as it would be if they had been taught sociology. The sociologist is often asked if he wants to kill off certain classes of troublesome and burdensome persons. No such inference follows from any sound sociological doctrine, but it is allowed to infer, as to a great many persons and classes, that it would have been better for society, and would have involved no pain to them, if they had never been born.

In further illustration of the interpretation which sociology offers of phenomena which are often obscure, we may note the world-wide effects of the advances in the arts and sciences which have been made during the last hundred years. These improvements have especially affected transportation and communication; that is, they have lessened the obstacles of time and space which separate the groups of mankind from each other, and have tended to make the whole human race a single unit. The distinction between over-populated and under-populated countries loses its sharpness, and all are brought to an average. Every person who migrates from Europe to America affects the comparative status of the two continents. He lessens the pressure in the country he leaves and increases it in the country to which he goes. If he goes to Minnesota, and raises wheat there, which is carried back to the country he left as cheap food for those who have not emigrated, it is evident that the bearing upon social pressure is twofold. It is evident, also, that the problem of social pressure can no longer be correctly studied if the view is confined either to the country of immigration or the country of emigration, but that it must embrace both. It is easy to see, therefore, that the ratio of population to land with which we have to deal is only in peculiar and limited cases that ratio as it exists in England, Germany, or the United States. It is the ratio as it exists in the civilized world, and every year that passes, as our improved arts break down the barriers between different parts of the earth, brings us nearer to the state of things where all the population of Europe, America, Australasia, and South Africa must be considered in relation to all the land of the same territories, for all that territory will be available for all that population, no matter what the proportion may be in which the population is distributed over the various portions of the territory. The British Islands may become one great manufacturing city. Minnesota, Texas, and Australia may not have five persons to the square mile. Yet all will eat the meat of Texas and the wheat of Minnesota, and wear the wool of Australia manufactured on the looms of England. That all will enjoy the maximum of food and raiment under that state of things is as clear as anything possibly can be which is not yet an accomplished fact. We are working towards it by all our instincts of profit and improvement. The greatest obstacles are those which come from prejudices, traditions, and dogmas, which are held independently of any observation of facts or any correct reasoning, and which set the right hand working against the left. For instance: the Mississippi Valley was, a century ago, as unavailable to support the population of France and Germany as if it had been in the moon. The Mississippi Valley is now nearer to France and Germany than the British Islands were a century ago, reckoning distance by the only true standard, viz., difficulty of communication. It is a fair way of stating it to say that the improvements in transportation of the last fifty years have added to France and Germany respectively a tract of land of the very highest fertility, equal in area to the territory of those states, and available for the support of their population. The public men of those countries are now declaring that this is a calamity, and are devising means to counteract it.

The social and political effects of the improvements which have been made must be very great. It follows from what we have said about the effects of intense social pressure and high competition, that the effect of thus bringing to bear on the great centres of population the new land of outlying countries must be to relieve the pressure in the oldest countries and at the densest centres. Then the extremes of wealth and poverty, culture and brutality, will be contracted, and there will follow a general tendency towards an average equality which, however, must be understood only within very broad limits. Such is no doubt the meaning of the general tendency towards equality, the decline of aristocratic institutions, the rise of the proletariat, and the ambitious expansion, in short, which is characteristic of modern civilized society. It would lead me too far to follow out this line of speculation as to the future, but two things ought to be noticed in passing. (1) There are important offsets to the brilliant promise which there is for mankind in a period during which, for the whole civilized world, there will be a wide margin of ease between the existing population and the supporting power of the available land. These offsets consist in the effects of ignorance, error, and folly—the same forces which have always robbed mankind of half what they might have enjoyed on earth. Extravagant governments, abuses of public credit, wasteful taxation, legislative monopolies and special privileges, juggling with currency, restrictions on trade, wasteful armaments on land and sea, and other follies in economy and state-craft, are capable of wasting and nullifying all the gains of civilization. (2) The old classical civilization fell under an irruption of barbarians from without. It is possible that our new civilization may perish by an explosion from within. The sentimentalists have been preaching for a century notions of rights and equality, of the dignity, wisdom, and power of the proletariat, which have filled the minds of ignorant men with impossible dreams. The thirst for luxurious enjoyment has taken possession of us all. It is the dark side of the power to foresee a possible future good with such distinctness as to make it a motive of energy and persevering industry—a power which is distinctly modern. Now the thirst for luxurious enjoyment, when brought into connection with the notions of rights, of power, and of equality, and dissociated from the notions of industry and economy, produces the notion that a man is robbed of his rights if he has not everything that he wants, that he is deprived of equality if he sees any one have more than he has, and that he is a fool if, having the power of the state in his hands, he allows this state of things to last. Then we have socialism, communism, and nihilism; and the fairest conquests of civilization, with all their promise of solid good to man, on the sole conditions of virtue and wisdom, may be scattered to the winds in a war of classes, or trampled under foot by a mob which can only hate what it cannot enjoy.

It must be confessed that sociology is yet in a tentative and inchoate state. All that we can affirm with certainty is that social phenomena are subject to law, and that the natural laws of the social order are in their entire character like the laws of physics. We can draw in grand outline the field of sociology and foresee the shape that it will take and the relations it will bear to other sciences. We can also already find the standpoint which it will occupy, and, if a figure may be allowed, altho we still look over a wide landscape largely enveloped in mist, we can see where the mist lies, and define the general features of the landscape, subject to further corrections. To deride or contemn a science in this state would certainly be a most unscientific proceeding. We confess, however, that so soon as we go beyond the broadest principles of the science we have not yet succeeded in discovering social laws, so as to be able to formulate them. A great amount of labor yet remains to be done in the stages of preparation. There are, however, not more than two or three other sciences which are making as rapid progress as sociology, and there is no other which is as full of promise for the welfare of man. That sociology has an immense department of human interests to control is beyond dispute. Hitherto this department has been included in moral science, and it has not only been confused and entangled by dogmas no two of which are consistent with each other, but also it has been without any growth, so that at this moment our knowledge of social science is behind the demands which existing social questions make upon us. We are face to face with an issue no less grand than this: Shall we, in our general social policy, pursue the effort to realize more completely that constitutional liberty for which we have been struggling throughout modern history, or shall we return to the mediæval device of functionaries to regulate procedure and to adjust interests? Shall we try to connect with liberty an equal and appropriate responsibility as its essential complement and corrective, so that a man who gets his own way shall accept his own consequences, or shall we yield to the sentimentalism which, after preaching an unlimited liberty, robs those who have been wise out of pity for those who have been foolish? Shall we accept the inequalities which follow upon free competition as the definition of justice, or shall we suppress free competition in the interest of equality, and to satisfy a baseless dogma of justice? Shall we try to solve the social entanglements which arise in a society where social ties are constantly becoming more numerous and more subtle, and where contract has only partly superseded custom and status, by returning to the latter, only hastening a more complete development of the former? These certainly are practical questions, and their scope is such that they embrace a great number of minor questions which are before us and which are coming up. It is to the science of society, which will derive true conceptions of society from the facts and laws of the social order, studied without prejudice or bias of any sort, that we must look for the correct answer to these questions. By this observation the field of sociology and the work which it is to do for society are sufficiently defined.

WILLIAM G. SUMNER.

November, 1882.

WAGES.

ONE may read, in scores of books and articles, that political economy is going through a transition stage. The inference appears to be that the period is a convenient one for any one who chooses to do so to contribute some crude notions to the prevailing confusion. It is certainly true that there is no body of economists engaged in carrying on the science of political economy by a consistent development of its older results according to such new light as can be brought to bear upon them. The science is exposed to the derision and flippant jests of those whose vested interest in old abuses is threatened by it, and it has forfeited its influence in the counsels of legislators and the cabinets of statesmen because those who call themselves economists are busy in turning economic science to scorn. Every science suffers more or less from men who meddle with it without mastering it, and from those who think carelessly, generalize rashly, or make concessions hastily; but a progressive science is always in the control, in the last resort, of a body of competent scholars who correct aberrations, and every such science possesses a body of criticism which is strong enough to repress presuming ignorance and charlatanism. Political economy is in no such position. A host of writers have been busy for the last twenty years introducing conflicting and baseless notions which, for want of a competent criticism, have won standing in the science. Others have made a boast of turning their backs on scientific method, and of describing, by way of contributing to political economy, some portion of the surface appearance which is presented by the mass of economic phenomena in their sequence, variety, and complexity. That is as if a historian should boast of abandoning the attempt to trace social forces in history, and of returning to the description of royal marriages and diplomatic intrigues. With all this the new school has been by no means moderate in its terms of contempt for all who did not accept the decree that Smith, Ricardo, and Mill were exceptional imbeciles to adopt and teach the old doctrines. I confess, for one, that for some years the writers of the new school imposed on me not a little by their airs of confidence and superiority. It seemed to me that I could perceive the errors into which they had fallen, the emptiness of their objections, the crude and unscientific character of their thinking; but I was forced to doubt and hesitate lest it might be I who was at fault.

For an example I will not take a small case or an extreme case. I will take an example of a very interesting and valuable book by one of the best living writers on political economy, but one who has, in my opinion, made unfounded and improper concessions on important economic doctrine. Leroy-Beaulieu[1] has not been able to escape the fascination of the longing for equality, and he declares his conclusion that Ricardo's doctrine of rent has no application at present because of the immense amount of new land which has become available, and that the Malthusian doctrine of population has no application because improvements in the arts are lowering the cost of subsistence in spite of the increase of population. Further on I shall notice some of the same writer's views about wages.

In the first place, the question What is true? is one thing, and the question of applicability to a given case is another. The former question is the one which is the concern of the scientific man. There is, however, another and more important view of the objections raised by the French economist.

In all our sciences we are forced to investigate ratios at the limit or other features of limiting cases. The older economists did this without having analyzed their processes sufficiently to classify them. The Ricardian law of rent is stated as a limiting case in the operation of the diminishing return from land. In any such statement the amount of land and the stage of the

[1] Essai sur la Répartition des Richesses et sur la Tendance à une Moindre Inegalité des Conditions, par Paul Leroy-Beaulieu. Paris: Guillaumin et Cie. 1881.

arts must be constant quantities. When the statement is derived from the limiting case it is used in political economy, as in all other sciences, by giving all values to the variables. Therefore the Ricardian law of rent applies to all cases whatsoever from Minnesota to Connaught. If we change the constants, either by getting more land or by advancing the arts, we produce no change whatever in the law, but only transfer its operation to another plane. As I regard it, M. Leroy-Beaulieu has fallen into the error of regarding a change in the constant as setting aside the law. The law of population is stated in terms of a limiting ratio between population and subsistence, land and the stage of the arts being constant. In its simplest terms the law is that the mortality and the increase of population are in equilibrium at the limit. M. Leroy-Beaulieu says that the law is set aside because we are not at the limit; but the law evidently covers all cases whatsoever, and to say that it does not apply is like saying that men are not under conditions of heat because they are not being either roasted or frozen. Whole libraries of books have been written, by way of criticism on the doctrines of political economy, whose argument consists in showing that human societies are rarely at the limit, or that limiting cases rarely or never occur. It seems to me, therefore, that the responsibility ought to be strictly enforced against men of standing in the science for concessions which introduce confusion, set the popularizers all astray, and make greater the task of those who are striving to secure the appreciation of sound doctrine. The men of the new school have scarcely met with any contradiction for the last ten years. They have had things all their own way. The effects of their teachings are to be met with in newspapers and popular writings. I am, however, one of those who believe that all this activity of the new school has been in the way of confusion and mischief. I do not doubt that we can to-day, with the aid of wider social philosophy and more careful study, expand and correct the doctrines of our science. We can advance it by an orderly and strictly genetic development. Any one who tries to advance it otherwise may be an apostle or a prophet; he is not a man of science.

I now propose to re-examine the subject of wages.

The origin of capital is lost in the obscurity which covers

the first beginnings of civilization. Some faint presages of capital are to be noted amongst brutes. We are told that a gorilla has been seen to take up a stick with which to defend himself when attacked. It is related that a monkey in a zoölogical garden used a stone to crack a nut, and hid the stone under the straw so as to have it ready on the next occasion. Beasts, however, with such extraordinary exceptions, live on the spontaneous products of the earth, which they consume as they find them, and which they obtain without tools or weapons. Such must also, at some time, have been the condition of man. In that stage of life alone could a man subsist on the immediate product of his labor. His labor consisted purely in an act of appropriation of the spontaneous fruits of the earth, which he consumed as he obtained them.

There is one tool-weapon given in nature—the flint; and there is one natural agent which man learned to use so early that we can find no period when it was not in use—fire. Accident was the leading factor in the earliest stage of civilization. All that we know of primitive men warns us not to believe that, if one man found a flint-knife, his comrades quickly took up the determination to acquire something of the same kind. The evidence all imposes upon us the conviction that the period during which the first steps towards capital, by the use of flints and fire, were being made must have been so long and painful that we cannot appreciate it. It is probable that steps forward were made only where population was dense enough to make effort necessary, and not dense enough to produce degeneration or distress. During that period the developments of rudimentary civilization must have been erratic and uncertain. Whenever any man or men, stimulated by perceiving the advantages which a man enjoyed who owned a flint-knife, and unable to conquer him and take it away from him, undertook to acquire one, not by accident but of set purpose, such persons were driven either to accumulate a store of food which would support life while searching for flints, or to go hungry while prosecuting that search. In either case the price of advance was the acquisition of capital by self-denial. From that stage of things up to the present moment it is true, leaving accident out of account, that *every step of advance by which man has raised himself above the level of other animals has been won by standing on a past self-denial, i.e. capital.* Capital is, like every other good, only a chance. Man may abuse it to his destruction or may use it for his advancement. That is where the moral deduction comes in, with which the economist has nothing to do, but the converse of the above proposition admits of absolute statement: Every diminution of capital lowers civilization without any possible alternative, and, in its measure, carries the race back towards the primitive barbarism. Labor and self-denial, to work yet abstain from enjoying, to earn a product yet work on as if one possessed nothing, have been the conditions of advance for the human race from the beginning, and they continue to be such still. From the beginning capital has been multiplied into itself in a constant involution. It is labor raised to a higher power and concentrated, and it is by this accumulation that man has gained the disposition of power enough, capable of concentration on a given point, to accomplish all his victories over nature. From the flint-knife up to the breech-loading rifle and the ocean steamer every step of the development is open to our observation, and not a single step in the sequence could be omitted or put in another position without making the result impossible.

The extension of our political economy which is most essential is the investigation of the element of *time*, and a specification of its value and relation in each of our generalizations. Already in the above sketch of the development of capital it is apparent that the relations of time are of the first importance. The work of mankind on low stages of civilization is irregular and unmethodical, but by the time that the agricultural stage is reached the successive periods of production repeat themselves with the regularity, because according to the necessity, of the seasons. Capital is the product of the past season. The work of the present season cannot go on without it, and it is not present unless the past period has been industriously employed. The future enjoyment, in its turn, depends on the industry of the present. The capital, moreover, in each period of production must be consumed; that is, used up and sacrificed. It must be sought again in the new product at the end of the present period of production, but in the interval it must be suffered to pass away and disappear. The element of risk therefore belongs to the nature of capital, and the work of mankind goes on in a series of pulsations in which the capital is consumed and sought again with increase in an endless series of reproductions.

On the hunting stage each man participates in the work and in the enjoyment. On the pastoral stage we already find cases in which men are left outside of any family connection and without cattle, the most essential form of capital. Such men, if not adopted into a family, and others who voluntarily take such a course, serve others who can give them a social status (security) and a share in the means of subsistence. In the early stages of the agricultural stage each man tills land for himself, and, so long as the land is abundant, new-comers simply take up more of it. In such a state of society, which is repeated substantially in all new countries, there is no class of persons who labor for others for hire. If any do this in their youth, or for a few years, they speedily acquire the small amount of capital necessary, in that stage of society, for tilling land, and become independent land-owners. As the population increases, however, the stage of the arts being assumed constant and land being taken constant in amount (viz., such an amount as is available for the use of a given society, whether it be, on that stage of the arts, a square mile or the whole earth), increments of subsistence must be won at greater cost of labor and sacrifice. The society is therefore forced to higher and higher organization because higher organization with differentiation of function increases production. As this movement goes on the society becomes more and more complex; the stake of each one in the stability of the organization is greater and greater, and whole classes arise which perform remote and incidental functions which would not exist at all in a less developed social system. In such a society a class of persons comes into existence who have no capital and no land. They must subsist from day to day out of the existing capital of the society by obtaining that capital from the owners of it through some form of voluntary agreement.

The English economists speak of the gain from the poorest land in cultivation as equal to current wages and profits. That they should have regarded wages and profits as positive data or known quantities is not strange in view of their situation and the circumstances of their country. There are in fact no positive data in economics from which results may be deduced as unknown are derived from known quantities. We have to accustom ourselves to think of the industrial system as in constant flux and readjustment. The elements of the system are numerous and are subject to constant variations in quantity and in their relations to each other. They are constantly moving, so that all forces which are produced in the system are distributed and taken up throughout the whole of it, so that every part is affected. A man of scientific training who studies society can no more doubt that this is true than he could doubt its truth as a general doctrine of the physical universe, altho society is more complex and its phenomena elude our investigation more completely. No doubt, taking a certain period, say a decade, into account, the existing ratio of product from the poorest land in cultivation to the labor and capital which must be expended on that land in the existing stage of the arts sets the general limit of the status of the lowest class of the population, from which the status of other classes is established in the proportion of what they contribute by their labor and capital to the total product of the country. In a new country where land can be tilled with a minimum of capital and a minimum organization of labor, any able-bodied man can obtain it and can win from it all the essentials of subsistence. To such a man the relation of wages to land is presented as an open alternative. There is no class, in such a country, of men who are driven, by the necessity of living, into a desperate competition with each other, without reserve, to get a share in the capital of the society. Women do compete with each other without the alternative. This is one of the chief reasons why their earnings are less than those of men in similar cases. In such a country there will be only an imperfectly differentiated wages class. The minimum of wages, where wages are paid, must be such as will give, all things considered, as good a return of comfort as can be won directly from the land. Since the latter return is great, wages must be high. Such is the state of the case at the present time in the United States. On the other hand, a country whose population is so great that the last increment of subsistence must be won from soils which require a great expenditure of labor and capital to win a meagre supply of the means of subsistence per head of the laborers must have a class of persons always on the verge of distress. As the use of such soils requires a large expenditure of capital, the laborers engaged upon it are employed by hire, and their status fixes a minimum of wages for manual labor.

Let us now vary the constants, the amount of land and the stage of the arts. It is plain that we immediately widen the margin of ease still further in the new country, and that we immediately relax the stringency of the situation in the old country. That is why civilization has advanced, and why we are now striving all the time to win progress in the arts. If the advance should be won as a single isolated step, it would bring relief for a time to all and an enlarged chance to all, but the law itself would not change at all; and if the population increased until it had absorbed all the advantage which had been won, the same results as before would be repeated. At the present time the unoccupied land of the earth is brought within such easy reach of all civilized men that there is no reason, save in the negligence of the classes interested themselves, why there should be any class of persons in the civilized world directly dependent on hire. The greatest mischief of all socialistic and semi-socialistic teaching is that it teaches the classes in question not to avail themselves by their own energy of the chances which are open to them, but to stay where they are and expect somebody else to make them happy there.

In a village community each man addressed himself directly to the soil to get out of it the means of subsistence. If then he failed for any reason whatsoever, he could only blame himself or nature. In our highly organized society we are all bound to each other in various relations while trying to win subsistence. The struggle for existence, therefore, which formerly had the character of a struggle of man with nature, now has the character of a struggle of man with man, and a "social question" arises whenever a man is dissatisfied with the return which he wins from the social co-operative effort. For instance: If a man were working by himself as a wheelwright and selling his wagons, he would have to put up with the best return which his labor and capital could win. If he could find any other trade which he could adopt and which would pay better, he would change. If, however, a capitalist employed wheelwrights and sold wagons, and if the trade should not bring back the capital and profits, the employer would either discharge men or lower wages. This is the form in which, under the social organization, the warning would come to the men that a redistribution of labor was required, but it would appear to them to be the act of the employer. Similar observations would hold of scores of other cases in which the ills of earthly life come to us as misdeeds of our neighbors towards us, on account of the relations in which we stand in the industrial organization.

Supply and demand, in the last analysis, are only so much need of subsistence and so many resources of subsistence, or, in other words, they are only the forms which are taken in the social organization by the original need of man addressed to nature on the one side, and the stores of nature open to the effort of man on the other. An isolated man would find the demand in his brain and the supply by his hand. When the supply had produced satisfaction the demand would arise again, and the reactions between the man and his environment would be repeated as long as he lived. In a primitive society a man who needed food exerted himself to get it from nature by some direct effort. A "just" return for his effort was—what he got. Under division of labor and exchange, even up to the last refinements of our modern industrial organization, it is still true that the society develops needs and addresses its efforts to nature to try to win satisfaction, but every man is forced to reach nature through a multitude of relations with his fellow-man. We stand in a double relation as suppliers and demanders around the one pile of goods which our organized effort has won from the earth and advanced into a shape to satisfy human needs. Hence every exchange involves two articles, each under two different relations. One article is supply to A and demand to B, while the other article is demand to A and supply to B. Hence demand and supply are the relations which bind men together into a human society for co-operation and high organization in a joint effort to win the supplies of life. The lowest terms to which any exchange can be reduced are therefore represented by two curves cutting each other; that is to say, by two simultaneous equations between two variables. Even then we have only a representation of an instantaneous transaction. If we take into account successive transactions and variations in supply and demand, we must introduce the element of time. We should then have to use the third dimension to represent the case, and after all we should have only an empirical, statistical, or, as we might call it, a statical, representation of supply and demand. If we should attempt any analysis of supply and demand regarded dynamically, we should also have to use the element of time ; and if we made such an attempt, we should find ourselves doomed to inevitable failure. It is not possible to analyze supply and demand. Why does A offer wheat for $1 and B bid only 99 cts. for it? These are secrets of the consciousness of the parties. One or both of them may be led by considerations which are erroneous. That will not affect the influence of his bid on the market. The economist can do no more than to note the bid when it is made as a contribution to the making of the price. The reasons for it he cannot discover. The most that he can do towards the analysis of supply and demand is to study the facts and circumstances which, by general tendency, go to make the supply of a given commodity, or the demand for it, greater or smaller. Indeed this is the only thing which it is of importance for us to know. Supply and demand are together the ultimate force or fact to the economist. They are to him what gravity is to the astronomer or chemical affinity to the chemist. We want to know the mode of their action, but the reason of it is beyond our reach. Supply and demand act to clear the market. If there were a closed market and a sale without reserve, supply and demand would just distribute all the commodities on the market. Supply and demand would not give each person what he would like to have, nor satisfy any ideal desires, any more than a man who addresses himself directly to nature in the first instance gets what he would like to have, but, if they act freely, supply and demand distribute commodities so that a given amount shall produce a maximum of satisfaction to the community between whose members the exchanges are made. At that point supply and demand would be in equilibrium and no further transactions would be made. In a simple society, with exchanges at country fairs, this state of things was reached. In our modern society, in which production, exchange, and consumption never cease, the conditions of the market constantly change and never cease, so that supply and demand move on towards an equilibrium which is never realized because the conditions of it are constantly changed. What then is "justice" in this connection? The distribution which takes place under the free play of supply and demand gives us our definition of justice as applied to the contribution which an individual puts into the social effort and the share he gets out of the social product. There is no other definition of justice which can be seriously considered.

There are two sources of confusion which must now be corrected.

1. The first is the definition of wages. If wages mean the remuneration of labor, then wages are a chief class, and we must distinguish between payment by the piece, contract wages, deferred wages, store pay, etc. etc., as sub-classes. If we make the definition of wages to fit contract wages, then the remuneration of labor will be a chief class, and we must distinguish between wages, payment by the piece, store pay, etc. etc., as sub-classes. Either classification is legitimate if it is faithfully observed throughout, but if any ambiguity is allowed to creep in it will produce the logical errors of a double definition and confusion between a chief class and a sub-class. These logical errors run through a great deal of the controversial literature about wages, and when they are cleared away a great part of the controversy falls to the ground. The second of the above classifications is by far the best, because it allows of a definition of wages which conforms to the popular use of the term. *Wages are a payment per unit of time by the employer, in return for which the employee agrees to use his productive powers during the time specified as the employer may direct.* I use the word under this definition only.

2. In the works of Mill and the other authorities there is a confusion as to the source from which wages are paid which is, I think, one chief cause of all the controversy which has arisen on this subject. It is distinctly taught under the head of wages that the demand for labor is capital, and that wages are paid out of *capital.* Under the head of distribution it is said that the *product* is divided into wages, profits, and rent, from which it

would follow that wages are paid out of product. Leroy-Beaulieu describes the employment of *capital* to sustain labor during production with great minuteness (pp. 366–70), and then declares summarily that the only "wage-fund" is "the total annual *production* minus what is necessary to maintain capital" (p. 382). Ricardo held that profits and wages are the leavings of each other. Later economists have generally rejected this doctrine, but even those of them who maintain that wages are paid out of capital fall back into arguments which imply its truth. For instance, Cairnes, who earnestly maintained that capital is divided into wages, raw material, and fixed capital, argued that trades-unions could not increase the wages in the several trades, because, if they did so, they would reduce profits below the rate which would make investment worth while. On his own doctrine, increased wages could not trench on profits. He should have argued that wages, if increased by a trades-union, could only be increased at the expense of raw material or fixed capital, which would be far more difficult than to increase them at the expense of profits. Indeed if the trades-union movement did not coincide with a new distribution of capital into its three parts (a new distribution which would produce a rise in wages), the trades-union could not possibly force an advance at the expense of raw materials or fixed capital. We shall see further on that wages and profits are not the leavings of each other, because they are not parts of the same whole.

If we could arrest the production and consumption of wealth in the United States at a given moment of time and take an inventory of all the wealth at that moment existing, it is evident that it would be an exact arithmetical quantity. It would be what the combined industry, economy, extravagance, folly, and idleness of all past time on the part of the American people had made it. It would be less because we have had a civil war, a protective tariff, a paper-money crisis, fires at Chicago and Boston, etc. etc., than it would have been if our public policy had been wiser and our misfortunes less. Whatever the existing wealth might be, no regrets could carry us back to increase it by a grain of wheat or a pound of iron beyond what it was at the moment supposed. This wealth would be divided by its character and by the disposition of it which was intended by the persons who owned it, in the then beginning period of production, into fixed capital, raw material, and supplies for the support of laborers. In one country, like England, the industrial system might be such that the support of laborers would nearly all be distributed in wages. In that case the term "wage-fund" might with great propriety be applied to it as a technical term to avoid a circumlocution. In another country, like the United States, the supplies for the support of labor might be, for the most part, owned by yeomen farmers and other independent laborers, or they might be distributed by other modes of remunerating labor than wages. A laborer may own a farm and support himself while working, and wait for his pay until the work is done. He then advances part of the capital and is not strictly a laborer only. He may take "store-pay." In that case he also advances part of the capital of the enterprise, and he goes into the market to borrow that capital, paying very heavy discount rates for it. These cases cannot throw any light on wages. They have to be noted only to eliminate them from the consideration of wages. The wages system exists, as above shown, only where the ratio of population to land is such that a class is differentiated which, having no capital or land, is dependent day by day for support on a contract relation with those who have capital. We have also seen that, above the very lowest stage of life, capital must precede and be the means to every productive effort.

In the actual period of production then, on a wages system, the existing supplies for laborers are distributed to laborers in wages while they, with the help of the fixed capital, till the ground and work up the raw materials, transforming the old capital into a new product. The risk, as we have seen, belongs to capital, and the great advantage of the wages system is that it leaves the risk all on capital. The laborer works by *time*, and when the time is over his contract is fulfilled. He takes no risk or responsibility. He is therefore at liberty to address himself to the accumulation of capital in the simplest possible manner, by economy of his wages, undisturbed by other elements. His share in the business lasts during the period of production and ends with it. He has no claim or right in the product, for he sold his share in producing it and took his pay for it during the process. The product is divided at the end of the period of production into the replacement of the capital (support of laborers, raw material, and wear of fixed capital), profits, and rents. As the capital to be replaced belonged to the capitalist, all the replacement goes to him together with the profits. Rent goes to the land-owner. The products are next distributed by supply and demand amongst all the members of the society, who turn them into capital and divide them, according to their good judgment, into the same parts as before, the product of the last period perhaps becoming the raw material of the next, and another period of production is then begun. If the product and profit of the last period were large, the accumulation of capital will be large—that is, the stock of supplies for laborers in the next period will be great; but it is not until the next period, and after an increase of capital, that any effect on wages can be produced. Hence it is clear that wages and profits are not parts of the same whole. Wages were in capital at the beginning of the period of production; profits are in the product at its close. We cannot establish any equation between the wages and the total capital, or the profits and the total product, or the total capital and the total product. How then can we establish an equation between wages and profits so as to determine the effect on one of variations in the other?

When now we have thus analyzed the operation in detail of the constant action and reaction by which the industrial functions of society are carried on, it is immaterial what may be the speed at which the process goes forward, or what may be the varieties of detail in different industries. Nothing can alter the nature or sequence of the forces and effects. The effect of credit to economize time and synchronize certain steps changes nothing in the scientific analysis of the process. It is a separate complication and refinement to be studied by itself.

Four inferences may be drawn immediately.

(1) We see that all questions whether the laborer gets his share of the product or not are, under the wages system, nonsensical. (2) That the appeal, often made in England, to workmen to take lower wages, so that the English products can be sold cheaper in foreign markets, are founded on false conceptions of wages, and ought to have no weight. (3) That the

arguments of the American protectionists, drawn from comparative rates of wages, are all fallacious. (4) That the attempt to connect wages with the price of products, by a sliding scale or otherwise, is founded on no true relations, and is doomed to failure. If an employer should say to his men, " My business is not prosperous like that of my neighbors. I want you to work for me for $2 a day, altho the market rate which you could get is $2.25,"—he would not deserve a respectful reply. Neither is there any sense at all in the demand of the men, if they say to the employer, " Your business is exceptionally prosperous, and we want you to give us $2.25, altho the market rate which we could get elsewhere is $2."

The notion that wages ever can be paid out of product is the most ridiculous notion which has ever been introduced into political economy. It would mean that a man who was tilling the ground in June could eat the crop he expected to have in September, or that a tailor could be wearing the coat which he was making. Men could then eat their intentions, wear their hopes, and be warmed by their promises. Even more than this: they might then believe that regrets were no longer vain, and having borrowed the future they could recall the past. The man who has been industrious to-day has a supper to-night. The man who has been idle to-day is hungry to-night. If wages can be paid out of product, the latter man, in his hunger, penitence, and regret, might as well obtain a loaf advanced from nature on credit to-night as to get one at any other time before he has won it by labor. He could then eat and sleep, and in the morning he could break his promise to nature and refuse to produce the loaf. Whenever nature yields to man an atom which he has not earned, or advances it one second of time before he has earned it, we may all turn socialists and utopists. The real gist of the question about wages lies right here. The " wage-fund " is of no importance one way or another. Every one who has yielded to sentimental faiths or longings to lessen the hardships of getting a living, or to discover some way by which men may attain to happiness except by conquering it, has seen himself forced to attack the doctrine that wages are paid out of capital.

Some instances of the fallacy about wages which has just been exposed are worth analyzing. In the July number of the

PRINCETON REVIEW Mr. Carroll D. Wright gives two cases which he makes the basis of deduction on the doctrine that wages are paid out of capital. The first case is stated thus:

"The workers are often the direct cause of the reduction in wages. This is well illustrated by circumstances within my observation. A well-known and prosperous dealer in boots and shoes in one of our large shoe towns is very popular with the workingmen because he will sell them a pair of boots for a quarter less than the same quality can be purchased elsewhere. It does not occur to them that they have paid that discount, but they complain to their employers who have cut them down—a cut-down required in order to furnish the popular dealer with goods at a low price to enable him to undersell smaller dealers. This retail dealer obtains from the manufacturer his lowest price for making one hundred cases as per sample. He then offers to pay so much—a sum less than the manufacturer's estimate—and pay cash. The manufacturer rather than lose a good cash order consents to make the goods, but not being able to reduce the cost of raw material takes the discount out of labor, and the workman berates the employer for reducing his wages while he praises the dealer for selling him his boots at a low price. Such circumstances often exist."

The inference which we are invited to make is that the workmen were foolish to buy where they could buy most cheaply because they thereby caused their own wages to be reduced.

In the first place, is the case correctly observed? If so, the employer-manufacturer sold goods by favoritism to one dealer who lowered his price to *all* his customers, and the employer lowered his wages for *all* his production so that his men had less to spend for *all* objects of their desire. The employer, therefore, in the last analysis, took something from his men and gave part of it to the general public of the vicinity and kept part himself, while his men lost on their wages what they gained on their shoes and more too. No one can regard such a statement as correct who has any conception of economic laws and relations. The true facts lie on the face of the statement. The reduction in price to the retailer came out of interest and insurance against bad debts, because it was given for cash. It did not have any connection at all with wages. It is to be assumed that the manufacturer would have given similar terms to any retailer who would have paid cash. Otherwise he would have been guilty of favoritism which would have ruined his business.

If wages were reduced, that act could not have had any connection at all with the fact that the employer had allowed to one customer a reduction for cash. Were, then, the men wise to profit by the reduction? Undoubtedly they were. Mr. Wright is driven by his view of the matter into the venerable fallacy that we get rich by what we spend, not by what we save, or that a demand for commodities is a demand for labor. That is really the fallacy at the bottom of all the unsound views of wages, but it is a certain extension of it to hold that the way for the men to make their wages large is themselves to demand a great many of their own products; that is, to spend their money freely.

Mr. Wright's second case is this:

"The day-laborer feeling himself more of a man than formerly must oftener wear a white laundered shirt, but he cannot pay over fifty cents for one. The demand of the higher civilization of the day-laborer must be met, and white laundered shirts are supplied at retail for fifty cents, and even for thirty-seven cents. But the wages of the women who make them have been reduced to eight cents per shirt. All such illustrations are simple, but well adapted to show the workingman what is meant by wages being paid from the product of labor, and in accordance with the profit which may be expected from the sale of the product."

What effect this proof of the effect of paying wages out of product may have on the laborer I cannot say, but I should think that it might arrest the economist by some misgivings as to his dogma. The fixed fact, the known quantity, in this case is "the demand of the higher civilization of the day-laborer." The day-laborer appears to be in command of the situation. He decides that he wants a white laundered shirt and that he only wants to pay fifty cents for it. Considering that he is the first man in the history of the human race who has ever been in a position to make his wants the law of his satisfactions, he certainly is moderate. As it is, his demand is satisfied by cutting the sewing-women down to eight cents wages. He might have called for shirts at a cent apiece, in which case the sewing-woman must have seen her wages reduced to two or three mills. He might have demanded boots at twenty-five cents, coats at fifty cents, cigars ten for a cent, and so on, and the wages of bootmakers, tailors, and cigar-makers must have come down in obedience to the law that wages come out of product, to the proper figure to satisfy his demand. Mr. Wright would be forced to argue that the way for the wages class to improve their condition is to buy each other's products freely at generous prices. I am a day-laborer myself. My higher civilization demands that I have a saddle-horse for five dollars and a cottage at Newport for a hundred dollars. If wages are paid out of product, I presume that, now that I have published my wishes, they will be gratified not later than next summer. As for horse-breeders and builders, let them look to their wages. I should like the cottage furnished.

The wild and untrained writers on political economy perform one useful function. They seize on all the fallacies and, naïvely and with good faith, perpetrate the *reductio ad absurdum*. Mr. George holds that wages are paid out of product, and that they are a portion only of the laborer's own product which the employer gives back to him. If this is true, it suggests three questions: 1. What is the difference between a slave and a wage-receiver? 2. Why is any man an employee? 3. Why is not every man an employer?

The rate of wages is determined, like every other case of value, by supply and demand. The total capital will be divided between wages, raw material, and capital by supply and demand. Capital, however, is limited by its nature with respect to the extent to which it may be transferred from one of these divisions to the other. From period to period the capital, when reproduced, is transformed into one or the other class by the dynamical operation of supply and demand.

From period to period changes in the arts, in the industrial development, in national habits, in fashion as to co-operation, etc. etc., will alter the proportion between the amount of capital paid in wages and the amount used to support laborers under other industrial organizations. The supply of laborers in one or the other mode of industry will also vary. Capital is divided between the wages system and other systems by supply and demand.

Changes in fashion, art, science, education, etc., will alter the relative importance of non-competing groups in industry. General changes will also affect the number of laborers in each of the non-competing groups. Capital is divided between the non-competing groups by supply and demand.

Inside of any one group the capital of that group will be distributed (in the absence of trades-union rules or other interferences) by supply and demand, according to the demand and supply of personal talents and capacities.

Some have inferred from the application of supply and demand to wages that the problem of wages was a simple case of a ratio, so much capital to so many men. The error here lies in applying a mathematical relation which is far too simple for the facts of the case. I have stated above what is the simplest mathematical form of an exchange under supply and demand. Obviously it is a great error to treat it as a simple ratio of arithmetical quantities, or even as a ratio of variables.

Others have turned away from the application of supply and demand with impatience. The Germans like to say of it that it is *nichtssagend*. Some of them put "law" in quotation when they speak of it. Any one who can sneer at supply and demand or regard it as a barren formula has certainly failed to understand it, or to study the scope and subtlety of its action. No one has ever analyzed supply and demand, regarded dynamically, because no one can. Leroy-Beaulieu says: "We cannot affirm that this formula [supply and demand] is false. We ought only to say that it is philistine and commonplace. It is certainly true, as Cobden said, that when two bosses run after one workman wages rise, and when two workmen run after one boss wages fall; but this sort of truism is not fitted to satisfy strict thinkers. What are the circumstances which determine the demand and the supply?" This last question he does not answer, nor even attempt to answer. It seems to me that a strict thinker proves himself by recognizing an ultimate scientific fact or law when he comes to it. The more one studies, the more one finds that the results of all studies are truisms. One is astonished that he did not see at once, by pure common-sense, the highest and last result of laborious investigation. If there is anything philistine and commonplace, it is to set aside the results of study as "truisms," and to pursue questions which can only lead off again into a maze of unclassified phenomena. Further on the same author says that in addition to the supply and demand of labor we must take into account the fecundity of capital. He urges that the demand for labor is a function not simply of the amount of capital, but also of its organization and activity. But in any given period of production any new activity or improved application of capital cannot act upon the wages during that period. The advantage will appear in the product of that period, it will swell the capital of the next period and then act upon wages. He then adds: "It is not proper to say simply, The more capital increases relatively to population, the more do wages rise. This proposition would be either inexact or incomplete, for the productive force may advance far more rapidly than the accumulation of material capital." This objection is not sound. If productive force increases, it immediately produces more capital. That is the proof that it has increased, and the mode in which the gain from increased force is realized. Advance in productive power is therefore followed by increase of capital within an interval of at least one period of production, altho further increase of capital, due to the same development of productive power, may continue to advance in a geometrical ratio through a long series of subsequent periods. New machines produce quick and approximately uniform increase of capital. Education or better government produce slower returns, which advance at a high ratio through a long period. The same author then comes to the " true formula " which he proposes "after having set aside the formulas and inflexible notions of the principal economists:" "The more production increases relatively to population, the greater is the chance that wages may rise." We have here a capital example of the necessity of separating the element of *time* in economic problems, and subjecting it to special study. We set out to find a formula for what determines the rate of wages, which is always a fact of a given time and place. We are offered a formula of the conditions of change in that fact between one time and another. Let us try a parallel. It is asked, What determines the weight of a man ? The answer is, Gravity acting on the mass of his body. No, M. Leroy-Beaulieu would say, that is a formula or inflexible dogma of the principal physicists. The weight of a man is determined by the fact that, if he has a good constitution, good health, good diet, obeys hygienic rules, does not work too hard, loses no limb by accident, etc. etc., his weight may increase from one time to another. Such errors would be impossible in any science but political economy, but recent economic literature is largely made up of just such confused thinking and reasoning. The rate of wages is the rate at which services are exchanged for means of subsistence under free contract and competition. It is therefore determined by supply and demand, like price, rate of interest, rate of foreign exchange, and all other cases of value.

We find therefore that there never ought to have been any "question" about wages at all, any more than there should have been a question about raw material or fixed capital. It is all wasted energy to re-analyze the subject and expose the fallacies which have been introduced by incompetent meddlers in economic science, encouraged by the concessions of the economists. Wages do not belong in distribution at all. They belong in the application of capital to production. The capitalist-employer is led by self-interest to try to keep wages down just exactly as he tries to prevent waste of raw material or wear and tear of fixed capital. The employee is led by self-interest to try to get all the wages he can. The struggle is legitimate and necessary. The result of it is that supply and demand distribute the capital amongst the laboring wage-receivers in the proportion which conduces to the maximum of production under all the existing circumstances. If trades-unions or employers' associations introduce interferences they may temporarily disturb this adjustment, but all such interferences avenge themselves in the end by compensating reactions. If a man knows how to earn more than he is getting, he ought to insist on getting more where he is or he should change. If an employer can get an equally competent man at lower wages, he ought to get him or lower wages. If we depart at all from this rule, we entangle ourselves in an endless muddle of sentimental rubbish, we lower production, and contract the welfare of all. There is therefore no "social question," or struggle of class with class, involved in wages. The notion that there is under "distribution" some new and unexplored field of economic science is entirely without foundation. That notion threatens to bring political economy still further under the dominion of metaphysics and sentiment, by the introduction of some notion of "justice," derived *aliunde*, as a controlling conception in economical science. It is indeed painful to think what an immense amount of poetry and declamation is swept away when we once get at the truth of the relations with which we have been dealing. If these relations were correctly understood, it would be impossible to make people any longer applaud the orator who finds it unjust that an industrious man is better off than a lazy one, or who wants a revolution because the man who has won capital by self-denial gets more luxurious living for himself and his children than the man who has spent as he went along. We should, however, have more sober industry and manly effort on the part of free, independent, and intelligent laborers to win capital and to put themselves and their children in a better position. There is no reason at all, at this moment, barring disease and accident, why any man living should not acquire capital, and, in view of the progress in the arts, there is no reason to apprehend, as far in the future as we can see, that this chance will not become rather greater than less for all who are prudent, industrious, and frugal, and who will turn their backs on the social doctors who have patent schemes for making everybody happy by setting those-who-have-not to rob those-who-have.

WILLIAM G. SUMNER.

www.ingramcontent.com/pod-product-compliance
Lightning Source LLC
Chambersburg PA
CBHW020248170426
43202CB00008B/273